T0316391

The Meetings Handbook

The Meetings Handbook

Formal Rules and Informal Processes

Ronald D. Francis and Anona F. Armstrong

ANTHEM PRESS
LONDON · NEW YORK · DELHI

Anthem Press
An imprint of Wimbledon Publishing Company
www.anthempress.com

This edition first published in UK and USA 2012
by ANTHEM PRESS
75-76 Blackfriars Road, London SE1 8HA, UK
or PO Box 9779, London SW19 7ZG, UK
and
244 Madison Ave. #116, New York, NY 10016, USA

British Library Cataloguing-in-Publication Data
A catalogue record for this book is available from the British Library.

Library of Congress Cataloging-in-Publication Data
Francis, Ronald D. (Ronald David), 1931-
The meetings handbook : formal rules and informal processes / Ronald D. Francis
and Anona F. Armstrong.
p. cm.
Includes bibliographical references and index.
ISBN 978-0-85728-451-8 (hbk. : alk. paper)
1. Meetings. 2. Business meetings. 3. Parliamentary practice.
I. Armstrong, Anona F. II. Title.
AS6.F68 2012
658.4'56–dc23
2012016976

ISBN-13: 978 0 85728 451 8 (Hbk)
ISBN-10: 0 85728 451 7 (Hbk)

This title is also available as an eBook.

CONTENTS

LIST OF TABLES

ACKNOWLEDGEMENTS

This work owes much to those who taught the authors about meetings. Their input over a substantial amount of time is greatly appreciated. Whatever may be amiss here should not be thought attributable to those whose generous advice and support was freely given. Those who anonymously provided samples of guide papers are also gratefully acknowledged.

The authors are particularly grateful to Professor Neil Andrews, editor of the *Australian Journal of Corporate Law* for his kind permission to use some of the material that the present authors published there. We are also grateful to the barrister, Mr A. Lang, for his useful comments on the manuscript. His expertise as editor of *Horsley's Meetings* makes his contribution most welcome.

It will be appreciated that this book was written by Australian authors and thus where no reference is made to a particular country it will be understood that the reference is to Australia. Notwithstanding, this work has been written with an international readership in mind.

Our thanks also go to the reviewers for their constructive comments, all of which have been appreciated.

INTRODUCTION

Meetings have been part of everyday life since the times of tribal and village elders. The notion of gathering for discussion is integral to social and political life, and is given various names – tribal meeting, *pow wow*, and, in the classical Greek *agora* or the Roman *forum*, orations and questions. They may be highly ritualised, as is the case of courts of law and of legislatures, or distinctly less structured, as is the case with meetings of the Society of Friends (Quakers), who speak when the spirit moves them. The latter approach would not work in so formal an organisation as a legislature.

The vigorous interchange that is so characteristic of legislatures, particularly in party politics, is such that a set of rules governing conduct is essential. It is interesting to note that the two most formal sets of procedures known to us are the legislature and the courts. In legislatures there is a vigorous interchange across the floor that would not be tolerated in court. It is left to the reader's imagination as to why there should be such a behavioural difference.

When the spirit (or the Chair) moves someone to speak, that person should preferably use plain language. Most people know that some language can be so inflated as to be incomprehensible. The notion of using plain language has many merits, and has an advocate in Asprey (2010). Unless there is a compelling reason, there is no point in using seemingly inflated language when plain English is both more concise and more comprehensible. There is a chapter in Asprey (2010) which he labels as 'overused words and formulas', including such a trite gem as '…do not hesitate to get in touch'.

One recalls the jokes about police language, using such expressions as 'I was proceeding at about 5 kilometres per hour in a westerly direction when I espied and apprehended the alleged miscreant'. Save where plain language might mislead (as may be the case in some legislation), exercising simpler terms – changing 'appurtenant to' to 'concerning', or 'exceeding, in excess of' to 'more than' or 'over' – allows stronger, more efficient communication.

The shared values and esteem, and of mannered consideration between those sitting on committees, are substantially fostered by adherence to the rules of civilised debate. Topics discussed in this book include essential formal rules and etiquette of meetings; basic ethical values that underlie social interchange; and courtesy and dignity, specifically how they substantially help forward the cause of the organisation.

A significant point here is that the values of formal procedures are conducive to personal enabling. Putting an emphasis on procedures ensures that the voices in meetings are equalised, which is essential to maintaining a diverse, balanced membership. In terms of the representation of disadvantaged minorities on committees and boards, Carter et al. (2003) concluded that, after controlling for size, industry and other corporate measures, there was a significant positive relationship between the fraction of women and minorities members, and firm value. As the proportion of women and minorities on a board increases, so does the value of the board to the firm.

Providing a formal framework, even if not always used, ensures that fairness – the right to be heard, to challenge the Chair and to insist on proper procedures – is an empowering fact. It ensures greater equality to every committee voice, and curbs the imposing excesses of voices that would otherwise dominate. In addition to formal procedures, other strategies of a less formal nature might be employed to facilitate committee work, to harmonise relations and to improve our quality of life.

Whether conducted formally or informally, discussion enables us to share collective wisdom, express divergent views, and seek consensus. Most importantly, it is a way of resolving issues that would otherwise be so contentious as to lead to fighting and war. As Churchill famously remarked, 'To jaw jaw is better than to war war'.

It is the complex interplay of ideas, the variety of perspectives, and the exchange of critique and support that make meetings so effective. As Waldron (1999) aptly noted, there is a collective wisdom that may well exceed the wisest counsel from the wisest man; a proposition philosophers have supported since Aristotle. Waldron called this the 'Doctrine of the Wisdom of the Multitude' (DWM). This theory was more recently affirmed by Ayres (2007), who noted that on *Who Wants to Be a Millionaire?* asking the audience produced the right answer on 90 per cent of occasions, whereas phoning-a-friend got it right on fewer than two-thirds of occasions.

However, group mentalities can be detrimental too. We need to be alert to 'confirmation bias', wherein people are more likely to critically accept information that confirms their belief. This 'herding' belief may act contrary to canvassing unconventional ideas; however, one of the advantages of meetings (when properly conducted) is that the less usual ideas may be advanced and discussed.

Most decision making in organisations does not occur in great leaps, but are incremental changes building upon past experience and endeavours.

Meetings are well suited to this type of decision making because the format allows input from all of those present. However, many are uncomfortable and self-conscious in a formal atmosphere and feel unable to speak freely, such that formality can discourage open discussion and debate. Yet without some degree of formality it is difficult to ensure that everyone has an equal opportunity to present his or her point of view, and therefore impossible to ensure that the outcome of the meeting has the support of a clear majority.

There is an important distinction between formal procedures and formal atmosphere. Formal procedures are essential for the proper conduct of the business of the meeting, but they need not lead to a strained or stilted style of debate. A skilful Chair, aided by members who are familiar with the rules of procedure, can relax the formalities without losing direction and control, and ensure that everyone present is at ease.

The rules and procedures summarised in this book have been developed over centuries as a structure within which the collective view of those present at a meeting can be clearly expressed. Even though many meetings are formal, some more so than others: still, meetings are human interchanges. In many cases, they even have the support of the law. Any person who is aggrieved by a decision of a meeting may bring a complaint if the accepted rules and procedures have not been followed. To be insensitive to fundamental human values impairs the effectiveness and dignity of the meeting. It is for such reasons that there are courtesies built into meeting procedures. Notwithstanding, there are still human relations skills that may be brought to bear.

There are some basic principles for conducting meetings. Among them are to not sit adversaries opposite each other, to always use courteous forms of address, and to not make accusations of improper motives, nor discourteously point out fallacious arguments. It is true that sometimes committee members play diversionary games. For example, during the proposal of an important, substantive issue, a member may ask a question such as 'Is the proposer perfectly happy with the use of the fused participle in the fourth line?' Such tactics are not designed to illuminate significant details, but rather to divert attention from the substantive issue, and to point ridicule at a proposer who does not know what a fused participle is, or why the distinction changes the meaning of the proposal.

This book addresses both rules and procedures – as well as, among other issues, how to manage the different roles of chairs and members, and how to manage the social processes underpinning much of the relationships and interactions that occur in meetings. It is particularly useful to members and committees of corporate boards, and includes many references to the corporate sector. However, the principles for achieving successful meetings are the same wherever people come together. People meet to achieve their common objectives in many different contexts: from corporations, to nonprofit organisations, to sporting organisations, to local neighbourhood watch groups. We hope that members of all types of meetings will be able to delve into this book whenever a problem arises, in order to seek guidance on how to respond.

Among the terms used in meetings that have become controversial is 'chair'. The Organisation for Economic Co-operation and Development (OECD) defines a chairman as a person chosen to preside over a meeting. In earlier times a meeting was conducted by a group in which only the master had a chair; the rest sat on stools or had no seats at all. This bestowal of rank has persisted in the language in the word 'chairman'. Attempts to avoid the male bias in the use of the term 'chair*man*' has led to attempts to find a term that applies to both male and female holders of the office. For a time the popular term was 'chairperson', but this does not easily role off the tongue. Today the convention appears to be to use 'the Chair' when referring to the office holder and 'Mr Chairman' or 'Madame Chair' when directly addressing him or her. In this book the authors have adopted this approach.

Most organisations have a constitution or memorandum of association, which sets out the structure of the organisation and the rules for holding meetings. Hence, the first part of the book, 'Structural Essentials', begins with a discussion of a constitution. Thereafter, we describe the different types of meetings, review the research regarding the composition of corporate boards, and explain the roles and functions of the Chair, the company secretary, and the members, including the expectations of each.

Following its formation, a meeting moves to the next phase in its development: introducing the formal rules for meetings. Such rules address what should be the composition of a committee; how to call and prepare for a meeting of the committee; and how a formal meeting should be structured in regards to the agenda, time management and the appropriate papers. These steps are described in Part One, followed by an account of the rules that apply to establishing a quorum, moving a motion and voting. An in-depth listing of the rules can be found in Part Five.

Part Two of this book describes the social processes and deep social structures that underlie the relationships and processes that complement the formal, visible rules and roles that take place in meetings. It describes the stages of development in groups that meet regularly, and advises leaders on how to manage the diverse behaviour experienced in meetings.

Another aspect of social processes is addressed in Part Three: the role that ethics plays in all aspects of our lives. This role is particularly important in meetings because a board or committee's approach to ethics sets the standard expected of members, and models the type of culture to be promoted within an organisation. If the board or committee condones unethical decisions, then it is okay for the rest of the staff in the organisation to act in a similar manner.

This book provides a number of resources to assist people in setting up committees or boards. These include, among others, a model constitution, and templates for an agenda and for minutes. These are included in Part Five of this book.

Part One

STRUCTURAL ESSENTIALS

The Constitution

The constitution of a committee or board sets out the purpose and functions of what it is to achieve. Some constitutions are brief, others quite lengthy. In addition to setting out the purpose and functions, the constitution should make clear any process that might be ambiguous: for example, whether a proxy should also be counted towards the quorum, or if all members are attending as delegates rather than as representatives. It is most important to clarify such matters in setting up the constitution in order to counter the notion that a rule is invented to fit a particular case. Such clarity can also prevent trivial arguments. For a sample of constitutions, see Part Four.

All committees require some rules to guide their internal governance. An organisation need not have a separate constitution of its own. It can simply take advantage of the rules provided by an outside organisation. For example, the Australian Corporations Law requires that companies must adopt the rules set out in the replaceable rules of the act, their own constitution or a combination of both. Typically the governance rules will deal with the appointment, removal and powers of an organisation's office bearers, the procedure for convening and conducting meetings of members and office bearers and rules related to managing the financial affairs of the organisation. The rules are set out in the constitution to meet the particular needs of the organisation.

Establishing and adopting the appropriate governance arrangements has two distinct advantages: it sets the standards of behaviour expected before any substantive issue arises, and makes the rules clear to all. A useful set of rules contains guidance on issues not addressed in the replaceable rules. An example is that, where it is appropriate, such as in breaking a deadlock, standing orders may be suspended.

It is important to note that a meeting or committee may only act on matters within the parameters of its power. If the group operates outside that power, it commits an act that is known in law as *ultra vires* (beyond the power). To avoid such *ultra vires* acts, a constitution is most desirable. Amongst other issues, a constitution defines what actions are within the powers of the meeting or committee. Notwithstanding what that constitution may say, however, the law always overrides what committees may do. For example, a few families cannot decide to secede from the state in which they live, and set up their own state: indeed there are plays based upon such fanciful situations.

Types of Meetings

People use the term 'meeting' in various contexts, with varying degrees of formality. The most formal meetings in Western society are those of the courts and the legislatures. There formality is essential, as judgements of fairness and due process are critical to outcomes. During a case of a national committee under the control of an attorney general, a meeting did not take place when it should have, and the decision of the attorney general prevailed despite due process. As a result, the decision was disputed as not having been properly debated, and therefore of dubious legality.

Committees and Boards

Committees and boards may take a number of forms. Boards of directors are legally responsible for decision making within a commercial company. The members of the boards may also serve on subcommittees such as remuneration, audit or succession committees. Committees and boards operate in an enormous variety of contexts ranging from those of multinational corporations to small, voluntary organisations. The spheres within which they operate may be commercial, professional, academic, research, governmental, or community.

Where there is no existing committee and there is a felt need, one could start a committee to start a committee. This is given the appropriate title of 'steering committee' (inaugural committee) – one that steers towards a properly constituted committee.

Committees may be deliberative or advisory. A deliberative committee deliberates and decides: the formal motions from deliberative committees are supposed to have concrete consequences. Where such committees are known and desired features, they may be called 'standing committees', as they have a specified and standing function that is essential to corporate objectives (an audit committee in a business corporation or an ethics committee for a research organisation, for example).

By way of contrast, there are advisory committees, whose name describes their function. When constituted by an act of parliament, in order to serve as a source of expert advice to government, these committees have the same legal responsibilities as a board of directors. Their place is to provide guidance and advice, which someone or some committee subsequently considers. In one case during a meeting, a deliberative committee resolved a particular point, and the Chair then thanked the members for their advice, thereby trying to turn a deliberative committee into an advisory one. It became plain after discussion that the Chair was not functioning properly due to illness, and had to be brought to order; this story also illustrates how alertness is essential to committee work.

Where a meeting for a particular brief has not met before, the meeting is, understandably, called an inaugural meeting. Apart from the formalities it is an opportunity to set the tone of the meeting. The Chair in particular, and members in general, have an excellent opportunity to develop a collective mindset, which can enhance their deliberations.

Types of meetings range in formality from the free-spirit gathering to the highly formal legislative assembly. Between these extremes are meetings in the commercial sector (from annual general meetings (AGMs) to the 'Monday get-together') and the public sector. Intermediate meetings may also be found in voluntary organisations, interest groups, and cultural and sporting clubs. Some of these groups may also contain subcommittees, which report to the main meeting.

Occasionally, participants of a meeting cannot physically assemble in the same location. One example would be a committee discussing issues regarding book production, or a formal document, participants are often in cities a long way apart. In such cases, it may be necessary to conduct the meeting by telephone or video-link, which can work well when used appropriately. Video-link is perhaps preferable, since at least the participants can see who is there, and what they look like – especially if they have never met. However, with present technology neither the images are as clear as on commercial television, nor the camera-work of the same standard. Often the camera is in a fixed position and thus does not track the subject appropriately. All that can be said is that it beats the alternative.

Another form of meeting, if one could call it that, is to have the Chair or secretary phone or email participants for their views. The severe weakness of that system is that it is not transparent, nor does it foster essential debate and interchange. Indeed, one doubts that one could call it a meeting at all. Although an initial contact via phone or email can be good for establishing views, agenda items, and the like, a meeting by one person canvassing cannot really be called a meeting.

Sometimes meetings may be joint meetings in which two separate committees or boards meet. That may be because some formal rule requires it (as is the case with some bicameral legislatures), or it may due to a common interest (such as buying a building that will be joint headquarters).

In Camera Meetings

In many commercial environments, *in camera* meetings – meaning those which are confidential and typically restricted to committee or board members, both executive and nonexecutive – are not only a normal part of committee or board meeting practices, but may be adopted within normal meetings, especially if a major decision is required. Best practice governance standards also suggest that meetings of independent or nonexecutive members be held without the CEO and executive members, so that participants can raise issues such as executive performance. Effective committees or boards often have private sessions on a regular basis, often before or after every meeting. Even if no supporting papers are presented during such sessions, members should still advise the Chair on the issues to be discussed.

Composition of the Committee or Board

The composition of a committee or board refers to its size (i.e. the number of members) and representation of diversity (i.e. the proportion of executive to nonexecutive or independent members; the qualifications of members; and the ages, genders and ethnicities represented). In some organisations, particularly in the professional and nonprofit sectors, members will be selected or elected to a committee from representative interests. It should be noted that such representatives owe their loyalty to the organisation to which they have been elected, and not to their constituents. Such issues of allegiance are often contentious.

Size of Committees and Boards

Regardless of size, a constitution may specify the minimum and maximum duration of committee or board membership, and the requisite qualifications thereof. Unfortunately, well-qualified people are in demand and may be appointed to several boards. An appointment of someone who does not have sufficient time to devote to their board duties, is inappropriate. The 'old boy network' (or *guanxi*, as it is known in parts of Asia) may be alive and well in many places, but that is no argument for depriving boards of a wider available talent.

When setting up committees, what is the ideal size? Research suggests that 10–15 members is the optimal size for a working meeting (Kiel and Nicholson 2003). Too few and there are not enough heads to ensure the quality of decision making, nor enough hands to complete the subsequent action plans that emerge from the meeting. Too many and there is not enough time for each member to contribute his or her opinion; if one complies with the notion that all interested parties should be represented, then one could end up with an unmanageably large committee. Small committees or boards of about a dozen members are most effective and efficient.

However, conflicting research has also found very large or very small committees or boards to be optimal (Coles et al. 2008). This especially holds true amongst organisations undertaking complex activities, which require more extensive monitoring. Further, there has been considerable research on the policies and rules regarding membership size (see Collins 2001). Restrictions on board size enhance company value; thus we conclude that there is a relationship between board size and financial success, although it is unlikely to be a simple one.

The number of participants has a major impact on the formality of a meeting. A large company's annual general meeting (AGM), which includes all the shareholders, requires a much more structured and formal meeting procedure than that of the half-dozen locals holding an AGM at their bowling or tennis club. Alternatively, a meeting of local residents, held on the same premises, that attracts a large number – such as an emergency meeting to oppose the proposal to build a freeway through the local sporting facilities – will require careful management of the procedures to prevent the high emotional content from disrupting the purpose of the meeting.

Qualifications of Members

Research has shown that there should be a balance of expertise and interests among directors and that these should match the skills needs of the organisation, whether it is for financial expertise, strategic planning or ethics (Wan Yusoff and Armstrong 2010).

The components that contribute to a board or committee's effectiveness include board members' demographic characteristics (age, tenure, multiple directorships), personality characteristics (integrity, open-mindedness), values (commitment, relationships) and competencies (experience in corporate management, relevant knowledge and skills, relevant types of educational qualifications) – as well as good networking with the government (Wan Yusoff and Armstrong 2010). In addition to member competence and diversity, further components that are important for board or committee effectiveness include clear roles and responsibilities, well-defined board structures and a good culture.

Diversity

Diversity of group membership can pertain to age, gender, religion, ethnicity, status, occupation, education or cultural background. While positive and powerful if managed effectively, diversity can be negative if discrimination and prejudice are allowed to take precedence over the potential benefits (McKenna 1999, 132).

We are all more comfortable dealing with people who are like us. This means that we are more likely to rate people more highly when they have similar characteristics to ourselves. Many years ago, when preparing an advertisement for new staff, one of us explicitly remembers saying, 'I want to employ someone like me'! When we seek our mirror images, we tend to devalue people from other backgrounds, and reject their opinions. This trend is often evident amongst people in power, who perceive their norms, expectations and behaviours as superior to those put forward by people of another gender, age or culture. In our heavily Anglo-Saxon society, a predominance of white males on committees and boards can enervate appointment decisions, group performance, and overall expectations for women and minority groups.

Groups whose members have similar backgrounds, interests, values, attitudes and so on are called homogenous groups. Groups whose membership is more diverse are called heterogeneous groups. Despite the fact that discrimination in the workplace on the basis of age, gender or ethnicity is illegal, the profiles of members in the top European, Australasian and American companies are fairly homogeneous. This may partially result from the high masculinity of many communities, which often instigates discrimination against women (Ely 1995). Today, women hold only 10 per cent of senior management positions. One wonders if some countries are losing the best of its female talent to the boards of companies located in other countries; of the few chairwomen in Britain, nearly all were born and educated overseas.

Homogenous committees and boards will have few difficulties with maintenance tasks, but may suffer performance limitations due to the narrow range of talents to contribute to decision making. They may also be limited in their capacity to lead companies whose major work force has an overseas parent, or whose consumer market is multicultural. When so many companies – even small business corporations – have global connections, lacking an appreciation and understanding of other cultures' expectations and needs can lead to poor decisions.

In contrast, groups with more diversity can often draw upon a wide range of skills and experiences to address complex problems. The big difficulty is that the more diverse the backgrounds and other attributes, the higher the level of skill required by the Chair to manage a meeting. However, the integration of committee members external to the organisation, where possible and appropriate, enhances the quality of the meeting enough to warrant the extra challenge.

Nonexecutive and Independent Members

Nonexecutive or independent members of boards are not in any professional or contractual relationship with the company, nor subject to outside influence or control in matters relating to the company (Pease and McMillan 1993). They should neither be substantial shareholders nor suppliers; nor should they have been employees of the company within the past three years. Furthermore, they should be free from any interest, business or other relationship that could interfere with their ability to act in the best interests of the company (Pease and McMillan 1993).

Nonexecutive or independent members bring new and different expertise to a company, and can offer independent advice on sensitive areas such as CEO appointments and remuneration. Such members serve to ensure that the company remains transparent, and that the actions by management are in the interests of all stakeholders. However, where inside knowledge of an organisation is required, an increase in the number of insiders, or co-option, can be beneficial.

The Role of Committee or Board Members at Meetings

Principles of good corporate governance identify different but complementary roles and responsibilities for the Chair of boards, the board secretary and the members (Armstrong 2004). The role of the Chair in preparing for and managing meetings and the relationship between the Chair and CEO are discussed more fully elsewhere in this work. The following section presents the formal rules applying to their roles in the governance structure.

The Chair

The function of a Chair is to chair the meeting. A competent Chair is well-prepared, and thus well-informed; knowledge is the basis of genuine leadership. The Chair is responsible for preserving order – for guiding the meeting through the agenda – and ensuring it follows the rules of procedure. The Chair's general responsibilities include ensuring that the views of members are adequately expressed and that any resolution reached by the meeting represents a majority decision. The Chair and Deputy Chair should be elected, unless otherwise specified, by the members of a council, board or committee (Clark 2005).

The Chair is entitled to the respect of members, and commonly not subjected to a vote of 'no confidence'. If the Chair's conduct of a meeting is unsatisfactory to a majority of members, a motion – that X take the Chair for the remainder of the meeting' – may be introduced, debated and voted upon. This motion has the status of a point of order, and must be accepted immediately by the Chair. If the Chair is vacated for any other reason, the meeting is closed, save an interim Chair be appointed.

The job description for Chair fits the Archangel Gabriel perfectly. Qualities indispensable to successful chairship include impartiality, tact, firmness and common sense. Without impartiality, for example, a meeting would not follow the conventions of reasoned debate and diplomacy.

A Chair requires an even more impressive character if appointed to the position by some outside authority. If not elected by the committee, the Chair may have to show that he or she is worthy of the position, and justify holding what may seem to be an imposed position.

Sometimes a committee will have an incompetent or malign Chair. The worst scenarios are either where the Chair is both, or where the Chair is competent but malign. Where there is incompetence and maliciousness, the former will manifest in the proceedings and the minutes, and consequently be able to be corrected. Where there is competence and maliciousness, however, correcting the Chair maybe more challenging, since it is harder to identify signs of hardcore maliciousness. Clever psychopaths are very difficult to counter because they often have cultivated social skills (Kiel and Nicholson 2003). How some of these issues can be addressed can be found in Part Two of this book.

With committee members the situation may be marginally better since a competent and benign Chair can lead the committee to reasonable conclusions despite. The writers recall one instance of a difficult member who never did what he promised for the next meeting and was habitually late. At the beginning of a meeting, when the Chair called for any special items, the proposal received and resolved was that X be confirmed or dismissed of membership depending on whether he produced what was promised. When X arrived, predictably late and without the promised material, he was advised of the committee decision, but was allowed to stay as an observer for that meeting only.

AGMs of large companies are mainly managed by the members. One of the difficulties here is that the Chair of the committee or board is also likely to chair the AGM: and, as such, has a proprietary interest in the proceedings. Skilled chairs could order the agenda, control the speakers, and generally work the meeting to their advantage. To counter this, one could commission an independent and experienced individual to chair an AGM, and ensure a nonpartisan meeting. Although this stricture may apply *a fortiori* to large AGMs, in certain circumstances it applies to small entities as well.

The secretary

The secretary is responsible for arranging meetings, preparing agenda papers, circulating all documents to members, and keeping records of meetings. These records, usually referred to as 'minutes', must record the date and place of meeting, the names of those present, and all the resolutions made at the meeting. Common practice is to record decisions made, but to omit discussion. The minutes have no standing as a record of the meeting until confirmed by members at the next meeting.

Approving the minutes is a not discussion item, save for questions of inaccuracy, misrepresentation, or omission. Anything arising from the minutes is dealt with under the item, with the self-evident title of 'Business arising from the minutes'.

During the meeting, the secretary takes notes, using these as *aides-mémoire* for the preparation of the formal minutes. A good secretary is a useful recorder and guide to the Chair, whose main attention is on running the meeting. As such, a skilled secretary is invaluable.

A 'company secretary' is secretary to the organisation as a whole as well as the board. As such, the position demands an intimate knowledge of the organisation and its procedures, and garners the close attention of the CEO, who often seeks the highly skilled secretary's advice.

Table 1.1. The roles of the committee/board, and members

Roles of the governing board

- Strategy formulation and approval – including the developments of major goals and strategies – in conjunction with the senior management team
- CEO selection, supervision, evaluation, mentorship, remuneration and, when necessary, removal
- Budget approval and capital expenditure
- Ensuring reliability of internal control: the procedural, financial and operational systems

Stewardship

- Ensuring funds are safeguarded, and getting used economically, efficiently and appropriately
- Overview of financial and material risk-management policies and procedures (relationship management of internal and external stakeholders)
- Monitoring organisational performance
- Acquisition approval and divestment strategies
- Balancing short and long term issues
- Appropriate and balanced reports to stakeholders (members and organisation, external interests)
- Exercising control in times of crisis

(Continued)

Table 1.1. Continued

Responsibilities: Meetings

- Attend meetings regularly
- Read background material and minutes
- Be willing to serve on committees
- Ask questions and contribute to the discussion
- Keep comments relevant
- Keep confidential information confidential
- Request and be open to feedback from the community, police members and other members

Responsibilities to other members

- Work as a team
- Represent the interests of the whole organisation
- Be willing to negotiate and compromise
- Respond quickly and effectively to issues/problems
- Anticipate issues/problems before they develop
- Be willing to set aside personal agendas
- Respond objectively to department and community
- Demonstrate discretion and common sense in communications
- Work as a team
- Model appropriate behaviour (manage conflicts of interest, and follow the codes of ethics and conduct, and disclosure)

Relationships with external stakeholders

- Be accountable
- Seek client/customer satisfaction
- Maintain internal and external communication
- Manage employee relations
- Respond objectively to stakeholders

Source: Muenjohn et al. (2010).

The board or committee

Board members have a number of different roles and responsibilities that require their attendance at meetings (Table 1.1). As well as working with other members of a board, a board member should also be engaged with external stakeholders. Their work on the board determines the effectiveness of their contributions to the performance of an organisation.

Commercial and other boards must (1) monitor the performance of management, and (2) add their value to the performance of the company. The compliance and performance roles have been recognised in several studies of corporate boards. Different aspects of compliance and performance have been associated with an external and an internal role (Tricker 1994).

Briefly, the external role is to provide accountability (compliance) through meeting government and nongovernment regulations; approving annual reports; and sustaining communication with various stakeholders. Internally the board contributes to strategy formulation by (1) endorsing the mission and direction of the company and the key actions to achieve its objectives, (2) auditing performance, and (3) approving the distributions to shareholders. These tasks are achieved through asking questions and offering insight about management plans and strategies.

Table 1.1 lists the roles of members, as drawn from previous studies and our own research. In addition to those of conformance and performance, committees and boards have other responsibilities too. Central to their role is the appointment and supervision of management; the stewardship of the company assets; and the responsibility of reporting financial and other events that impact company performance.

Good relationships between members enable the group to work as a team – interacting to address issues without giving way to personal agenda. Teamwork includes following the codes of conduct, which prescribe how to manage conflicts of interest, and modelling the behaviour that sets the norm in the company.

Accountability to the external stakeholders, employees, customers, creditors and communities in which a company operates is increasingly important as external parties intrude more and more into company domains. While legislation addresses many of these relationships, the ability to give objective consideration to stakeholder issues is not only an ethical, but also a risk-management issue.

Separation of committee / board and management

Despite the role of a governing committee or board in confirming an organisation's strategic direction and objectives, there is overwhelming support for the conviction that the roles of boards and managers should be separate. A board's role is to establish policy and oversee performance, to promote and protect shareholders' interests – not to operate the company. Their role is to work with and through the executive team. This corresponds to Tricker's view (1994) of the internal roles of the board, i.e. to monitor (compliance), and develop future-orientated policies (performance).

Committee and board balance

As indicated above, corporate governance standards suggest a balance of executive and independent members. Similarly, best practice governance standards suggest that the roles of Chair and CEO of an organisation not be exercised by the same individual; further, they suggest appointing an independent member or director as Chair. Of course, in small or family companies, the Chair and CEO are often the same person. In Asia, where a large proportion of companies is family dominated, independence is assured by appointing a chairman separate from the CEO, as well as other measures (Chen and Nowland 2010).

Another reason to keep the role of Chair and CEO separate is that the Chair requires a significant time commitment, and other positions might attenuate the Chair's performance. At present, a substantial majority of commercial directors sit on more than one board. Selecting directors or members from a limited pool can lead to interlocking directorships, which place potential limits on independence.

Formal Rules

The essential formalities of meetings ensure economy of time and resources, and fairness of debate. They are a major means by which the equitable contributions of all are accommodated. Without a proper knowledge of the formalities on the part of all participants, a meeting could become ineffective or subverted. Yet this book argues the need for not only knowledge of formal procedures, but also sensitivity towards the human element in meetings. Civilised conduct in meetings is not only worthy in its own right, but also conducive to efficient decision making and speedy process. It also enhances the quality of both business and social life.

Much of corporate behaviour is governed by formal decisions made in formal meetings, where governance issues are debated and resolved. The purpose of these meetings and their consequent decisions is to emphasise the role of formal meeting procedures in advancing honest corporate objectives. Corporate governance is about the direction and control employed in organisations, as well as the organisation's accountability. Such responsibility and authority with regards to the organisation's direction and control rest with the committee or board.

Corporate governance, in its many and various forms, is exercised, controlled, and made accountable through formal processes. Notwithstanding, it is imperative to recognise that many meetings operate on a consensual basis. The rules exist as a fundamental position to be used as a resort when consent fails. As such, there is a need to set guidelines as to the conduct of meetings. Furthermore, that the rules should be in place in advance of problems, rather than invented to suit each particular occasion, deserves substantial emphasis.

One of the present writers served for ten years on one committee. Being a substantially consensual operating committee, only once during that time did an issue come to the vote. As the issue polarised the committee, the Chair, quite rightly, went to formal procedures to resolve the matter. What is important here is that everyone understood and accepted that the rules were designed to resolve such impasses, and all members readily accepted the outcome.

We understand that, realistically, many meetings are consensual rather than formal; what is important is an understanding that when consent fails, then there is recourse to the agreed formalities by which such disputes are to be resolved. Even though the rules may not be applicable all of the time, it is essential that there be a basis for resolving contentious issues in a collegial manner.

Milhaupt and West (2004) canvass the notion that, for Japan, both formal and informal rules should govern not only corporate meetings, but the economy as well. As they put it:

A seemingly technical and innocuous legal change sparked a huge increase in shareholder derivative suits/actions brought against the directors by one or more shareholders on behalf of the corporation to redress a wrong against the corporation itself and changed the scope and mechanics of shareholder monitoring in Japan.

Some meetings have a regularity that is clearly understood. For example, an AGM is clearly annual. Extraordinary general meetings (EGMs) are, as the name implies, extraordinary and thus called in a manner determined by the constitution. Other meetings may be of the 'we always have a meeting on the first Tuesday of the month' kind. Just because it is customary does not make it essential that the meeting take place. If it does not, all those involved need to be clearly informed about the reason why. Here is good guiding principle: have the meeting scheduled, and cancel if necessary, on the grounds that cancelling is far easier than instituting a meeting. Further, one might accrue some credit for cancelling as the news may come as a relief from what is, to some, a burden.

Calling a Meeting

In order for meetings to be legal – and to ensure that everyone is well informed about the agenda – a period of notice needs to be given, commonly no less than seven working days in advance. A committee or board meeting may be declared invalid if any member complains that he or she had not been notified of its taking place. Placing an advertisement instead of advising each member individually is not usually acceptable; however, a meeting to which the general public is invited may be called by advertisement. Notice of a meeting should provide details of the business to be conducted – an agenda in some form. In the case of a public meeting, which is usually about a single issue, a simple statement of that issue is sufficient. The general point is that appropriate and understandable notification of a meeting must be made.

Meetings should be called only with advance notice in writing: either by mail to the last known address, or by email with a read receipt required. In addition to informing those invited of the duration of the meetings, invitees need to provide adequate advance notice so that appropriate preparations may be made. Without such preparation, members are signally disadvantaged, as Doucet (2007) outlines. Doucet also avers that the Asian approach to meetings is one of extra preparation and consideration, and has fewer elements than in the Western approach, where meetings are sometimes used to canvass ideas rather than create structured interchange. Without an appreciation of such conduct in Asia, Westerners may be disadvantaged in crosscultural meetings.

One must be aware that different cultures have different attitudes towards meetings. Whether they are formal or informal interchanges, or whether they entail relatively aggressive or mild disagreements, is determined not only by the character of the meeting, but also by cultural expectations. Without appreciating such cultural nuances, some may be disadvantaged in crosscultural meetings.

That justice delayed is justice denied has long been an accepted precept. Without a time limit on decisions, one can play extended games that kill ideas simply through the attrition of time. Indeed, Bell (2002) notes that delay tactics have prevented the passage of certain US legislature. Further, such tactics may be used to wait until the appointment of particular judges before referring certain matters. They may even be used to extend a court decision long enough for private interests to engineer the next election in favor of a particular aspirant to the bench (at least in those places where judges are elected). Such is the basis of a Grisham novel, *The Appeal*. Setting deadlines for certain events can prevent such unethical behaviours, and act as a valuable tool for accomplishing goals.

Conflicts of interest can also undermine the integrity of a meeting. We define conflicts of interest as cases where a fact, perception or point of view compromises professional objectivity. It is a firm, guiding principle that members declare any conflict of interest before an issue is debated; further, it is advisable that they dismiss themselves from the meeting while the issue is being debated and resolved. Family ties and crossdirectorships may be relevant and should be disclosed.

It is the expectation that each individual member is an independent entity. Notwithstanding, there is a perception, justified or not, that members related by blood, marriage or sexual liaison do not act as independent persons.

Where the relationship has been established before appointment, the time to challenge is before the related individuals are appointed to a committee. Where the relationship develops after appointment, the time to challenge is at the recognition of the relationship. Difficulties can arise when a head of an organisation allows a related person to take on a significant role, in that there is a conflict between being professionally aware of operating principles and overcoming the difficulty of asserting oneself to the head of the organisation concerning the behaviour of the related person. A useful ploy here is to establish some firm principles beforehand, and then adhere firmly to them.

It is a well-established convention for the Chair to request disclosure, and to record potential and actual conflicts of interest prior to beginning the meeting business. Included among potential conflicts to be disclosed are memberships of other committees or boards, and sources of income. One of the resources in Part Four is a guide to recording conflicts of interest.

Conduct of Business

All business should be handled by motion. Each motion should be proposed and seconded (any motion that does not find a seconder thereby lapses). The Chair invites the proposer to speak first, and then the other members. This interchange usually gives rise to a debate of the pros and cons. From the discussion it may emerge that the motion would be more acceptable if it were amended. The Chair would then invite someone to propose an amendment.

If an amendment is acceptable to the proposer and seconder, it must be introduced before the original motion is put to a vote. The amendment must be in the spirit of the original motion, and must not negate or nullify the original motion. An amendment takes precedence over the original motion and, if carried, becomes the new motion before the Chair. If it is defeated, then the original motion stands. If it is accepted, that amendment is then put before the board; if carried, the next motion is that the amended motion becomes the substantive motion, and debate ensues, culminating in the amended motion being put to vote.

Interruptions of speakers should only occur when there is a point of order: when calling on a quorum, or a move to closure, or proposing that the speaker no longer be heard, or that strangers be excluded. All these points of order are effectively procedural motions. The committee may, of course, determine other procedural motions to foreclose on speech be formalised. For a list of procedural motions, see Renton (2000).

Items of business to be dealt with at a meeting should appear on the agenda in a regular order. A fairly common order suitable for use at most meetings is to begin with opening and apologies. The minutes of the previous meeting are put up for approval and/or amendment, followed by business arising. This is followed by the set of substantive motions; the handling of any other business not previously addressed; the determination of the date of next meeting; and the closure of meeting.

In the UK there is a rule called the Chatham House Rule (Chatham House being the home of the Royal Institute of International Affairs in London). This rule is expressed such that, in any meeting, 'participants are free to use the information received, but neither the identity nor the affiliation of the speaker(s), nor that of any other participant, may be revealed'.* This seems an admirable precept. It is, however, up to the group to decide on the governing principle.

The notion of confidentiality is an interesting one with respect to meetings. Here one of the issues is to what degree the confidentiality of the deliberations should be kept. At one extreme is the notion that anything said in a meeting may be revealed and attributed to the speaker. At the other extreme is the notion that only formal resolutions may be recorded, without the names of proposers and seconders, and with restricted circulation of the minutes.

There is a case to be made that the deliberations are not to be reported, but that who voted for what is reportable. Yet too ready an identification of speakers, of who said what, may be inhibiting to some. Clearly, the decision as to what maybe revealed is, in large part, up to the committee itself, using its own terms of reference.

The extent of confidentiality of commercial board meetings is a debatable issue. On the one hand, confidentiality ensures healthy, open debate. Effective boards must act together as a team, making decisions, providing leadership and confirming the corporate strategic direction. In effective boards and committees, trust binds the team together, feelings are expressed freely, and creative tension enhances group performance. On the other hand, there is the question of whether or not stakeholders have a right to know what is going on in the committee room.

Any disclosures have a number of components. Among them are the act of disclosure, the actor, the subject of disclosure, the target, the recipient of the disclosure, and the outcome (Jubb 1999). There is always a balance to be sought between transparency and accountability, and business competitiveness and confidentiality of the committee.

When members are in meetings they may have a deeply held belief that, for example, abortion is proper in some circumstances – or they may believe that it is sinful in every situation. When in meetings, members will have a

---

* See http://www.chathamhouse.org/about-us/chathamhouserule-translations (accessed 23 May 2012).

good idea of their nonnegotiable position (for example, that a dangerously low standard of safety is unacceptable). An outline of some of these principles may be helpful, particularly when dealing crossculturally (for an account of such principles, see Parts Two and Three).

Some meetings are held in confidence (as one might find in a university faculty committee where students' results are considered); others are open meetings where anyone interested may attend (as in a local government monthly meeting). Further, there is the question of whether or not the press may attend a particular meeting. It is helpful here if the constitution has a ruling, and also if the committee or board makes its position clear.

Committees operate as a whole. The implications of this involve the right to ask questions and to speak freely without being called to individual account by outsiders; the notion of cabinet solidarity should apply. Suppose that member X was the only one to speak against a certain motion on an issue dear to his or her heart. It would be improper to have someone report that member X was the only one to oppose a particular motion. Within a committee members must be free to ask questions, to pursue particular lines of inquiry, and to vote according to evidence and conscience. Once a decision has been reached, it is the committee's view, and not that of an individual. All committee members stand behind what has been properly resolved.

The Agenda

The agenda has some informal aspects to it, which we address in Part Two of this book. Agendas must have some set structure, but there is still room for interpretive manoeuvres. The opening part, for example, is fixed: establishing the Chair and those present, proxies, acceptance of the minutes of the previous meeting, business arising, etc. The end of the meeting attends to 'any other business' and designates the date, time, and place of the next meeting. Within these parameters, it is possible to structure the agenda in such a way as to put like items together to make a general point, or to separate items in the expectation that like items may be seen to be connected.

It is possible to pad the agenda – to intentionally make it longer – in order to achieve a preferred outcome of a particular motion. Placing an item at the end of a long agenda can be done in the hope that members will be too tired to care when faced with vigorous debate, and will relinquish their positions to the wily and persistent member who thus wins the motion.

A meeting agenda is the notice paper of items of business to be dealt with at the meeting. A common mistake in preparing the agenda is to provide a list of items without indication of what is to be done with them, and without supporting information. Members should be given the opportunity to be fully informed on the issues before the meeting, and should be provided with a recommendation for action. While the meeting may decide not to accept the recommendation and proceed to do something quite different, the inclusion of a recommendation focuses attention on the issue, and indicates what kind of action should be considered.

Agenda items that are not controversial, but require committee approval, may be starred for consideration. Some items, such as approval of previous minutes, must be discussed and therefore are typically starred. Other items that are not obligatory to discuss may be left unstarred. Where any member wants an item starred, the Committee does so – thus no item may be omitted on which a member wishes to speak. Any remaining items left unstarred may then be adopted as a whole (such as by asking, 'May I have a motion that all of the unstarred items be accepted?'), thereby shortening the agenda by disposing of uncontroversial items.

Sometimes a set of proposals is so linked that it could be possible to treat *en bloc*. If there is no objection to bloc treatment, it is a way of advancing through business in a rapid but seemly manner.

Managing the Agenda

Most meetings begin with apologies, followed by the minutes of the previous meeting. It is currently common to record the decisions and pertinent issues, such as actions to be taken, and to avoid details, such as noting 'who said what'. A good strategy is to distribute the minutes in writing prior to the meeting. Any corrections or additions to the minutes can then be received by the secretary and incorporated. The Chair seeks confirmation of the revised minutes, and signs them. Matters arising from the minutes may then be addressed if they are not incorporated in the agenda items to be discussed later in the meeting.

Minutes of subcommittees come next. The Chair of each subcommittee should provide draft minutes of meetings, and present a three-minute oral report on the major issues. This approach keeps the subcommittee chairs accountable and the members informed. Attendance at committee meetings is open to every member of the committee/board. If there is a presentation from an executive or other expert, that person's slides should be distributed before. PowerPoint presentations are often overused and can waste valuable time. The number of slides should be limited to three or four; discussion and question time tends to be more illuminating.

Guidance on the Chair's role in managing discussion within the meeting is provided more fully below. In brief, the Chair manages time, keeps members focussed on the key points, and curtails digressions. The Chair's role is to facilitate the meeting, not to give a monologue on personal views or issues.

If the Chair wants to do that, the Chair should temporarily step down and hand over the position to another member.

A meeting is a bit like a meal; the chef (the Chair) should make sure there is an entrée (beginning agenda, papers, purpose, appropriate roles for participants), a meal (the contents, processes) and a sweet (positive achievements from the meeting, tidings or steps about the next meeting). The Chair should bring each item to an appropriate conclusion with a decision or recommendation, and ensure that the secretary is clear about the item's inclusion in the minutes. If the last agenda item is 'other business', it is courteous to advise the Chair of any items for the next meeting so that they are not raised without notice.

After the meeting, the Chair may resolve any administrative matters with the secretary, and may hold a brief discussion with the CEO, in order to progress matters that arose from the meeting.

Minutes

The minutes of a meeting are the official record of what was debated, and what was passed. It should give the facts of which committee met, what date and place the meeting occurred, who was present, what apologies were stated, what proxies were announced, etc. As previously noted, the minutes are not regarded as an official record until affirmed at the next meeting. This allows for any errors to be corrected. For examples of minutes, see Part Four.

Delegate and Representative

One may be aware of mindsets among committee members. One form that this might take is that of being either a 'delegate' or a 'representative'. Committee members may be appointed to represent their organisation on the board of another organisation, such as a national body. They are vested with the power to make decisions based on the evidence and arguments presented at a meeting. When appointed to a board the decisions must be made to reflect the interests of the organisation to which the board belongs, not those of the organisation which they represent and who appointed them.

An extreme example is a small company debating giving bonuses. The pros and cons may be debated in a meeting, including the issue of whether it is better to leave that money in the business in order to strengthen commercial viability; or devote it to employee welfare; or use it to make capital investments in the company. One could readily imagine a union representative asserting that the money should go to employees, no matter what the arguments in favour of alternative spending. The difficulty is that such meetings are not really informing and debating forums; rather they are vehicles for affirming entrenched positions. As such, perhaps we should have a term that differentiates affirming from debating committees and boards.

All members of committees and boards should have their powers delegated so that they can listen, debate, form an opinion, and vote accordingly. It is, therefore, more appropriate for all committee members to be there as delegates rather than representatives. No matter what instructions are given to members who represent a vested interest, all members are expected to contribute and benefit from the debate, and to vote accordingly in the interests of the committee. Members of a committee or board should have, as their priority, the interests of the committee or board that they are attending. If they represent an interest group, they must still act in the best interests of the committee that they are attending. To do otherwise would make nonsense of the committee process, as predetermined interests are not amenable to argument and evidence.

There are legal precedents for this view. For example, the Supreme Court of New South Wales, in the case of *Bennetts vs Fire Commissioners of New South Wales* ruled in 1967 that a board member owes first allegiance to the committee or board on which s/he sits, and not to the organisation that s/he represents. One would expect that most jurisdictions would come to the same conclusion.

Motions

Meetings proceed by way of substantive motions. As the name implies, such motions are matters of substance (for example, that there is approval of the accounts). The other kind of motion is a procedural one. All substantive motions should be in the affirmative because a negative motion, if defeated, leaves the meeting in doubt as to what has been resolved. For example, the motion that members have their stipend increased by 10 per cent is clear; the motion that members are not to have their stipend increased by 10 per cent is ambiguous – this could mean that it will be, for example, increased up to 20 per cent instead, or else decreased or left unchanged. Motions must not only be clear but also unambiguous. For example, 'that John Brown be appointed as Chair' is both clear and unambiguous, while 'that John Brown be nominated as Chair' is clear but ambiguous as a motion; the latter is merely a nomination whereas the former is clearly intended to have a practical outcome.

There are occasions in debate when it is appropriate to foreshadow a motion, thereby showing that the foreshadowed motion is both relevant to what is to be determined by the motion that is on the table, and helpful to members in making up their minds about a particular issue (this process even has a pretentious alternative name – adumbration). For example, one might be nominating a CEO for a new position, and a foreshadowed motion might be that the new CEO be appointed for a period of no less than three years in order to give them time to achieve a particular set of commercial circumstances.

A motion to rescind a decision – known as a 'rescission motion' – is not generally accepted at the meeting that made the decision in question. The reason behind this policy is that time for reflection about the implications is needed. Notice of such a motion, to be introduced at a subsequent meeting, is usually required. There should be firm guidelines regarding rescission motions.

In contrast to substantive motions, there are also procedural motions. Convention recognises several procedural motions – sometimes referred to as 'formal motions', owing to the fact that they are formal procedures for dealing with common occurrences at meetings. These motions include such issues as the imputation of improper motives to a committee member; the assertion that the current speaker is not addressing the motion; or the request that the debate on the motion be adjourned. Procedural motions of this kind are intended to facilitate the conduct of business. Points of order are similar to procedural motions, designed to ensure that the meeting follows the proper order – hence the points. A point of order might be, for example, that the committee is considering an issue on which they have no power to determine, or that the Chair has made a ruling from which the committee wishes to dissent.

As mentioned, a point of order takes precedence over all other business, and should be dealt with immediately. The ruling of the Chair on a point of order may be challenged by a motion of dissent that has been proposed and seconded. Another member of the meeting should be asked to take the Chair while the motion of dissent is debated.

A point of order may be raised by any member of a meeting at any time. The person raising a point of order should indicate clearly to the Chair that he or she is doing so, and should receive the Chair's immediate attention. A point of order takes precedence over all other business, and should be dealt with immediately. The importance of a point of order is that it ensures that the procedures of the meeting are followed: that fairness is kept by following the rules.

A statement or question by any member, broached with the permission of the Chair, does not infringe upon that member's right to speak for, or against, a motion. The Chair may allow someone to make a point (perhaps of information) that will inform the debate. However, when a member poses a question, there is the knotty problem of what constitutes an answer. Such replies may range from a 'decline to answer' or some obfuscation, to a clear and helpful response. The constitution should therefore address the subject of questions and answers. For example, it might hold that 'all questions posed by members require a direct answer to a direct question'.

Rights and Responsibilities of Members

A member of a meeting has the right to propose and second motions, engage in debate, and vote. In some cases, a category of nonvoting members exists. Such members are usually permitted to engage in debate and raise points of order, but are not permitted to propose or second business motions, or to vote. All persons present at a meeting are entitled to (1) an equal opportunity to contribute to debate, and (2) protection against abuse, defamatory statements, imputations of improper motives, and allegations of improper conduct. All persons present at a meeting are expected to observe the rules of procedure and conduct themselves in an orderly manner, and to observe the authority of the Chair.

A member who is entitled to vote has the right to have his/her dissent from a decision of the meeting recorded in the minutes. This valuable option means that if a member disagrees strongly with a motion that has been passed, his/her dissent is recorded in the minutes, so that later that member cannot be accused of supporting a motion at odds with his/her conscience. For useful references, see Gunther (1987), Paul (1995), Lang (2006) or Milligan (2007).

When someone is appointed to a committee, it is expected that he or she will attend and contribute. It is not unknown for someone to accept a committee membership solely in order to add the title to his or his list of accomplishments, without actually caring to contribute to the committee. In such circumstances it is appropriate to replace that person with a more active and committed member. To this it may be proposed that nonattendance in person for a given percentage of attendances be grounds for dismissal from the committee. It would beneficial, if such a policy is implemented, to have it stated in the constitution, and in the rules of meetings.

Suspension of Standing Orders

When the meeting needs a lift or a diversion from formal procedures, there is a device known as 'suspension of standing orders'. A suspension of standing orders allows free discussion of any matter. The usual rules of procedure are relaxed, and members may speak freely before the committee. No motions may be introduced until standing orders are resumed. Usually the Chair suspends, and resumes, standing orders. The decision to suspend or resume standing orders is, like much of chairship, dependent upon a certain social sensitivity and insight. It is such insight that makes good Chairs so highly prized.

Voting

Voting is the formal means of reaching a decision. (Reaching a decision through consensus is discussed elsewhere in this book.) Voting should normally be conducted by voice or a show of hands, but any member may request an anonymous poll. Votes should then be in writing, collected by the secretary and given to the Chair. This is a useful device where there is a contentious topic, or an exceptional need to preserve objectivity. Commonly a secret ballot is done when a member calls for one. Secret ballots allow a conscience vote without offending. Members can use them to get a free vote without being embarrassed or annoyed at being identified as voting a particular way. A scrutineer or scrutineers may be appointed. When votes have been counted and checked, the Chair announces the result to the meeting.

A voice vote, or even a show of hands, may lead to ambiguity in the decision. For that reason, any member may call for a formal count; this ensures that the correct decision is recorded, and that members are satisfied that it is as recorded.

It is common practice to allow the Chair both a deliberative and a casting vote. The latter vote is usually cast to break a deadlock. The Chair may also exercise a casting vote against a tied motion. An example in which such a vote would be appropriate would be in a tied motion of an amendment, because it would keep the original motion before the meeting. It is a useful convention, though not a requirement, that a casting vote defeats an innovative motion, unless there is a good reason for innovation. This preserves the continuity of the motion and the gains of the status quo.

A motion is passed when a sufficient number of votes are recorded in its favour. A majority is a common standard, but there are occasions (as, for example, when a body corporate wishes to sell some common property) where a larger majority is required (perhaps two-thirds). The constitution should state which forms of voting are employed (first-past-the-post, preferential, weighted, casting, etc.), and in which situations.

Quorum

A quorum is the minimum number of members required to be present before any business can be conducted. Unless otherwise specified, it is usually accepted that a simple majority of members entitled to vote constitutes a quorum. Whether the acceptance of a proxy (with the member being absent) is considered as part of the quorum, however, needs to be resolved within each committee. Wily committee members may work the quorum rule to their advantage. We have seen cases where a member is opposed to a motion that is likely to be passed. That member excused himself from the meeting, and notified the chairman that his departure would result in the absence of a quorum – thereby buying time.

For any vote to be binding, it must be determined by a quorate committee. In the absence of the minimum of members to vote, any motion passed is not binding. Thus a quorum is defined as the minimum attendance necessary in order to pass a motion. It is an obvious but important point that definitions should be given where there is any prospect of ambiguity. Here one would need to define 'attendance'. Does, for example, the existence of a legal proxy constitute 'attendance' by the member who gives the proxy, and can thus be part of the quorum?

Proxies

Where proxies are given, it is necessary that they be given in writing and signed; proxies should be explicit rather than implied. Without such a safeguard, someone could falsely claim to be a proxy for another member. This overtness can also help resolve any later dispute about who held whose proxy.

A further complication with proxies is that a person may be properly given the proxy holder in order to press a particular point on a substantive issue. It should be clear to the proxy holder that he or she represents another, and must (or need not) forward the absent member's views. Arguing forcefully for a particular view on behalf of someone else does not negate the central issue that all members of a committee or board must then vote according to the arguments and evidence adduced – and not as blind followers of instructions.

When a proxy is given, it should be understood that the person receiving the proxy is a delegate – someone who listens to the argument and then votes according to conscience, evidence, and argument; it is not someone who is instructed to vote a particular way regardless of the circumstances. To do so would be to make meetings meaningless (see above). One of the main points of meetings is to talk, listen, and be persuaded. A proxy is given by one member to another on the understanding that he or she is in tune with the issues that may be involved, and will vote according to the argument and evidence.

It may not be relevant to all committees or boards, but there are some motions that do require more than a simple majority. Consider, for example, motions such as 'that the accounts be received', or 'that a dividend of X per cent be declared' that may require a more consensual vote than a just over 50 per cent. For example, there may be occasions in which a motion may only be passed with a majority of 75 per cent. Such occasions should be specified well in advance in order to offset the possible criticism that such a decision was ad hoc, and designed only to block a particular motion.

The appointment and reappointment of directors needs a formal motion, which may require that each director receive a separate motion in order to prevent a bloc declaration.

Recording Resolutions

If all voters vote, and all vote the same way, it is called 'unanimous'. If not all vote, but if those who do vote choose to vote the same way (i.e. with no contradicting votes), it is called '*nem con*' (*nemene contradicente* – no one contradicting). If a motion is passed and a member wishes, they may have their dissent recorded formally in the minutes. This ensures that, at no future time, may a member be accused of voting for a motion that is later seen to be unworthy (see above).

Time Issues

On principle, neither an individual nor an organisation can bind its future self. That being said, committees will honour agreements made earlier. If a decision needs to be undone, then the proper way to undo it is to have a rescission motion, with considered debate. It is much the same with legislatures. If a particular government has a treaty or an undertaking, a future government will honour it – with the right to negotiate, amend, or invalidate it if the circumstances warrant (as in declaring a war, for example). The essential point is that there has to be continuity, with the recognition that this is a changing world.

Because of such policies – designed to sustain values like continuity and equality – another aspect of meetings, often contentious, is that they might occupy indeterminate time. Strictly following a firm agenda is one way of ensuring that meetings feel less interminable, and do not go on too long. Another method is to put pressure on members. There is a story of a former mayor of New York, whose council was deliberating one winter about some social issue to do with the homeless. To facilitate an apt solution, the mayor had the heating turned off, whereupon a speedy conclusion was reached.

One might even employ the convention of the British Privy Council, which holds meetings with members standing (this seems to bear no relationship to the previously mentioned point that the master has the chair and the rest either stand or sit on backless stools). It is told that the convention began when Queen Victoria, recently widowed, became determined to reduce her public duties to a minimum. Or perhaps it began as a mark of respect to the Prince Consort. Whatever its origin, the idea certainly makes the point about being to the point.

Perhaps a rule about the length of meetings should be included with those of other time and date elements; for example, 'The meeting will be held on 24 February 2010, starting at 3.00 pm and finishing no later than 5.30 pm'. Thus we might invert Parkinson's Law and hold that a meeting's work contracts so as to fill the time available. (This reference is to Parkinson's (1955) work, in which he devises a law that states, 'work expands to fill the time available'.) This is patently true of meetings, many of which go on beyond reasonable time simply because they are meetings. If we were to hold that 'agendas should contract to fit the time available', it would help to focus deliberations and prevent time wasting. It is not suggested that all meetings so conform, however, for some issues do require extensive and careful debate.

There is an apt expression in law that 'justice delayed is justice denied'. Unless heard within reasonable promptitude, there is no justice. Indeed, some professions – accountancy in particular – have a precept in their code of ethics holding that a failure to perform certain actions within a given time frame constitutes an ethical breach. In law, however, an action could be delayed until the litigant dies; a foolishness analogous to an alleged pregnancy testing service with a nine-month wait time.

Urgent versus Important

On the matter of conserving time, it is apposite to remember that time is a precious commodity, and not something to be squandered. From a psychological point of view, our perspective of time is a crucial element of our makeup. Those who are future oriented tend to wear watches, smile more and laugh less than those of the here and now. Those who dwell in the expanded present are obviously less time-bound than those who dwell in time. Those with a historical bent may be of quite a different character as those future oriented (Zimbardo and Boyd 1999).

Time orientation is intimately connected to our sense of what is important and what is urgent. Covey (2004) provides an analysis of the urgent-important dimension. As he notes, urgent is not the same as important. It may be important that we plan our career, but it may not be urgent; it is urgent that we decide to drive around an obstacle on a one-way street, but whether around the right or the left side may not be important. In this we need also to recognise that some things are both urgent and important (such as deciding whether to respond to an attack) – and some things neither urgent nor important, such as an atheist's opinion on the doctrine of transubstantiation.

Closing Comment

When a meeting convenes, it has several functions to fulfil. One is that of open and informed debate, with a view to coming to a decision that is well articulated and well informed, and that results from varied, expert input. Many committees and boards need to debate in order to formalise a decision. While the process of reaching a decision is not a rubber stamp metaphorically, a physical stamp is applied, giving an official imprimatur to the decision. Such stamped conclusions and decisions have some legal force; it is, therefore, important there be preceding debate, and that the voted conclusions are commercially and ethically defensible. For a more detailed account of ethics, see Part Three, and Francis (2009).

Many meetings operate on a consensual basis. The rules exist as a fundamental position to be used as a resort when consent fails. The essential formalities of meetings ensure economy of time and resources, and fairness of debate. They are a major means by which the equitable contributions of all are accommodated. Without a proper knowledge of the formalities on the part of all participants, a meeting may become ineffective or subverted.

Such knowledge is particularly important for meetings in which the dividend return is critical to a livelihood. As such, it is incumbent upon the committee or board to demonstrate fairness and insight, which it partially achieves by the existence, circulation, and consideration of the rules of meetings. Civilised conduct in meetings is not only worthy in its own right, but also conducive to efficient decision making and speedy process.

This book argues that the rules for formal meetings are an indispensable adjunct to fair dealing, good personal relations, and good corporate governance. The rules for formal meetings derive from centuries of experience, and are designed to foster rational debate and relevant information. Even though we recognise that most meetings operate on a consensual basis, the fact that there are fallback rules is crucial. When consensus does not work, everybody should know how the issue will be resolved. Various national corporation acts provide tacit consent to the importance of this principle.

It is worth recording that we do not need to assent to everything, only to the propositions under consideration. For example, one might assent to the conclusion to make the quorum 'more than half the members', but not to worship in a church of the Chair's choosing. As Waldron (1999) notes, 'consent does not carry physical force; it carries rather moral force with regard to the purposes for which consent is required'. Ultimately, formal procedures govern all meetings, and thus it is essential that the rules of engagement be set beforehand. The use of an agreed set of rules or an authority set out beforehand prevents time wasting and destructive argument from hindering resolutions on contentious issues.

Part Two

INFORMAL PROCESSES AND SOCIAL MATTERS

Introduction

Research that supports the principles presented in this book that govern the discourse on meetings is drawn from a variety of sources. A body of psychological and management knowledge is focussed on human relations in general; management research into groups and teams; and, more recently, in the context of best practice corporate governance, roles and attributes of members, and how they impact the responsibilities and behaviour of the participants in board meetings.

Psychological research into human interactions and relations in organisations has been developed over decades. It includes studies of personality characteristics and 'types', and of relationships between people. Personality 'types' have been constructed from observations of various forms of behaviour. Examples of characteristics include extraversion – associated with active, sociable, assertive people – which contrasts with introversion – associated with reserved and quiet people. People also differ in whether they feel that their actions are controlled by external factors, or whether they are 'internals': that is, people who exert control over their actions and lives.

Belbin (1993a) used the research scales of introversion and anxiety/stability to produce four types. Stable extroverts excel in jobs that place a premium on liaison work, and where co-operation is sought from others; anxious extraverts are commonly found where people need to work at a high pace and exert pressure on others; stable introverts work well where good relationships with a small number of people need to be maintained over a period; and, lastly, anxious introverts exhibit self-direction and persistence, and are often found among creative people. In further research Belbin extended this approach in order to examine teams, where he identified seven roles that are characteristic of people working in teams.

Belbin also researched the personality characteristics of successful Chairs. He concluded from his research that the outcome for companies, in terms of financial results, depends largely on the personality attributes of the Chair. Successful Chairs are positive; trusting by nature; accepting of people as they are, without jealousy or suspicion; dominant; committed to achieving goals and objectives; calm and unflappable; practical; gifted in the extravert capacity to motivate others; and yet prone to detachment and distance in social relations. However, Belbin also found that, on average, successful Chairs are not more mentally able or creative than their less successful counterparts.

The Machiavellian personality is typical of people who endeavour to control and manipulate others. They hold cynical views about other people's motives and are always seeking political motives for behaviour. They concentrate on personal goals, even if reaching them requires unethical behaviour. Ethics are addressed in Part Three of this book.

It is inevitable that there will be mavericks on committees. Being as they may be advocates of unpopular causes, they need to be nurtured rather than ostracised. Without such people, the world would be duller – less experimental – and would make less progress. The drawback of such a harsh treatment of deviants is that it reduces social diversity and tolerance; it also reduces civil liberties in society, and deprives modest dissenters from enjoying the benefits of the right to be different.

People in organisations spend most of their time with other people – in conversations, meetings, committees (Kotter 1985; Mintzberg 1973). The complexities of their relationships extend well beyond this book. Social interactions in groups, and therefore in meetings, are influenced by values such as competition, control and self-protection. According to Bolman and Deal (1991), these values are ingrained in a political view of the world where resources are scarce, and competition and conflict are dominant features of organisational life. In groups, this political perspective shows itself in the development of coalitions with different values, preferences, beliefs, information and perceptions of reality. Because conflict is inevitable, power becomes the most important resource.

Conflict in groups can be both positive and negative. From a positive perspective, conflict challenges the status quo, stimulates interest and curiosity, and produces new ideas and innovative resolutions to problems (Bolman and Deal 1991). In contrast, when people withhold their views to avoid uncontrollable conflict, trust erodes (Senge et al. 1996). The lack of trust and manipulating behaviours discussed above often lead to conflict in meetings.

Some studies look for these negative aspects of conflict rather than for positive ones. Feindler (2006) for example, examined human interactions by looking specifically at anger management techniques. A countervailing approach is Compton's (2005) work, in that it attempts to take us away from negative emotions.

The practical benefits of understanding the rules which govern behaviour have received attention: Chase (1953), for example, emphasised behaviours that impact commercial and industrial efficiency, as did Hodgetts and Hegar (2005). Mantovani (2000) wrote on exploring cultural borders, and how our culture frames our behaviour and organises our experiences; and Branscombe and Doosje (2004) on collective guilt and its consequences.

There are studies that address the rules that govern behaviour within particular subject areas: Kurtz et al. (1985) wrote on issues amongst counsellors; Mosvick (1971) on scientists, technicians and engineers; Harzing and Ruysseveldt (1995) on the internationalisation of human resource management; and Stroh and Johnson (2006) on an organisational psychology human resources guide. Reece and Brandt (2005) wrote on human relations in an organisational context giving organisational and personnel applications.

Bolman and Deal (1991) assert that conflict will be more salient and intense in times of adversity and in groups with greater diversity. Since conflict is an inherent part of managing groups, a question that this section of the book addresses is how the misfit can be identified, and how conflict can best be managed to take advantage of its positive potential and avoid its dysfunctional aspects.

Kotter (1985) believes that, when planning meetings, the politically astute Chair needs to address three areas: (1) the setting of the agenda; (2) networking and forming coalitions; and (3) bargaining and negotiating. The formal aspects of setting the agenda were addressed in Part One, and some of the informal aspects will be addressed later in this section, Part Two.

Networking and coalition building prior to meetings have been extensively studied. Kotter (1985) suggests that the four basic tasks are, first, to identify the relevant relationships; second, to assess who might resist cooperation and why, and how strongly (an analysis of stakeholder interests and expectations can be useful here); third, to develop relationships with people who can facilitate the negotiation, education or negotiation processes, and deal with resistance; and fourth, when step three fails, to carefully select and implement more subtle or more forceful methods.

Another relevant area of research is into the informal and social processes that take place in meetings. Knowledge of the processes, or group dynamics, that take place in meetings, is grounded in research into teams and groups. This research originates a long way from company boards. It is grounded in research into workers, specifically how they are motivated to work together to achieve better performance. The scientific management school (Taylor 1911) assumed that dividing work into simple and specialised tasks would result in more control over production, require less skilled workers, and lead to greater profitability. However, the negative psychological effects of depersonalisation, and feelings of alienation and frustration leading to poor mental health and low product quality, soon became evident. It became increasingly recognised that a group's achievements and performance depended not only on achievement of production, but on the interactions and social motivation in groups.

In the 1960s and 70s, research focussed on team development (Tuckman 1965; Schein 1985). By the 1980s, Moss Kantor (1983) and others were heralding the importance of working together as a team at all levels in an organisation. Belbin (1993b) and Margerison and McCann (1990) identified the different roles that people take in effective teams. In the next years, specific roles were also identified among members of committees and boards. Leblanc and Gillies (2005), in their study of Canadian companies, found that interactive processes, director characteristics, and structure are important for effective performance. They described the behaviours of five roles taken by 'functional' directors, and the corresponding roles of 'dysfunctional' directors. Senge (1995) raised the profile of teams to the executive level when he advocated team learning as the 'fifth discipline' required to achieve a learning organisation – one that is committed to continuing improvement. He defined team learning as 'the process of aligning and developing the capacity of a team to create the results its members' desire' (Senge 1995, 236).

Senge wrote that committees and boards need to be made up of more than just talented members, and do more than just share their vision for their company; they need to know how to work together, to align, because almost all important decisions in companies are made by teams, either directly or through the need to translate individual decisions into action.

This chapter addresses the way in which today's members work together through the skills of dialogue and discussion: understanding how to manage the difficult 'defensive routines' individuals use to avoid conflict, and how the Chair takes a major role in managing difficult meetings. The benefit of an effective team is a dynamic which can bring the collective and diverse set of the skills of the members to bear on the important decisions. As Kiel and Nicholson (2003, 279) note:

> Good corporate governance depends on the board wielding collective authority to communicate policy and strategic directives forcefully and unambiguously to the top management team. Having a collective responsibility means that everyone works for the good of the organisation and has a shared vision. Only an effective team can address wider policy and strategic issues.

This leads to the final area of research that contributes to the understanding of meetings: research into corporate governance. Such research permeates this book. The major governance theories that apply to meetings are agency theory and stakeholder theory (Clarke 2004). Agency theory is based on the premise that, because the owners of companies (i.e. shareholders) are separated from direct control of their companies by the managers (their agents), there is a need for mechanisms to control the managers, monitoring their performance and ensuring their accountability. This view drives the guidelines and codes of good governance (Armstrong and Francis 2004a, 2004b), which recommend the independence of boards, including the independence of the formation, structure and composition of boards of directors, and of the attributes of their members; and the separation of the positions of Chair and CEO. Stakeholder theory holds that companies owe responsibilities to a wide range of stakeholders that not only include shareholders, but employees, customers and the wider community. An essential premise of stakeholder theory is that corporations should be socially responsible.

Both theories have an impact on meetings. In Australia, corporations laws set out the structure of boards and the regulations applying to meetings (Francis and Armstrong 2009). These are evident in Part One of this book. This section, Part Two, addresses the relationships between boards, their members and other stakeholders, and the social dynamics of these relationships. While other chapters in this book are about formal structures and procedures involved in meetings, this part is about some of the informal, but often equally important, processes and social interactions that take place in meetings.

Despite all their potential hazards and difficulties, meetings serve a useful function in most organisations. Their purpose is described in Part One of this book, followed by a description of how to prepare for an effective meeting. The effectiveness of meetings can be improved by understanding the processes that occur before, during and after meetings. Preparation includes determining the content, order and pace of the agenda, and making available the relevant papers. Group dynamics are the processes operating in groups which affect both the maintenance of the group relationships and interactions, and the group performance. When committees or boards are newly formed, the members need time to learn how to work together as a team, to recognise their individual strengths and reach a stage where the business of the board is conducted efficiently. In contrast, the focus of this book is on the stages of group development, the progression of group decision making, and the role of the Chair at each stage in a board's development as an effective team. Associated with these processes in groups is the matter of how members communicate.

Why Should We Hold A Meeting?

Meetings take many forms depending on the purpose or task; the number and characteristics of participants; the relationships between participants; the degree of formality in the procedures; and the roles of participants. A meeting may be held face-to-face, but corporate meetings are increasingly conducted via teleconference or videoconference.

Meetings provide a context for interaction. They are held between two or more people. (It is very difficult to hold a meeting of one!) How formal a meeting will be depends on the context. A meeting of two lovers at the seaside is quite informal, as are family meetings held between a husband and wife with or without their extended family. The formality is very different, however, when a meeting is held after a funeral, in order to hear grandad's will read out by the family solicitor.

However, the focus of this book is meetings in organisations. Meetings in organisations serve both informal and formal functions. Formal functions have to do with the task for which the meeting has been called to serve. They provide:

- A means of working on a complex task that cannot easily be undertaken either by any one individual or by a number of independent individuals, that is, where independence is important;
- A means of generating new ideas where information is widely dispersed, or where mutual stimulation enhances creativity;
- A liaison/coordination device, particularly if the group includes members from the various parts of the organisation to be coordinated;
- A problem-solving mechanism, particularly if the issue is complex, requiring inputs from a range of perspectives;
- A means of facilitating the implementation of decisions; and
- A means of socialisation, where a common message and a common perspective are reinforced.

Informal functions serve a different purpose. They are the processes where the focus is on group maintenance and interpersonal dynamics (Bion 1961; Schein 1985; Bales 1970). They meet the needs of individuals attending the meeting, as well as those of the group as a whole. They serve as:

- A means of fulfilling social needs, i.e. needs for friendship/social interaction;
- A means of developing, enhancing and confirming a sense of identity/self esteem;
- A means of establishing and testing beliefs and understandings. Developing shared meanings through shared experiences and shared discussions;
- A means of reducing feelings of insecurity, anxiety and powerlessness; and
- A mechanism for accomplishing problem-solving tasks for informal objectives.

If a meeting serves none of these purposes, then there is potential for emergence of some of the undesirable processes and outcomes discussed further below. A meeting may be a one-off event or an ongoing coming together of members at regular intervals to accomplish a task. A board of directors that meets regularly is an example of the second kind.

Organisational meetings are usually formal in structure, but can be very diverse in terms of type. They range across a variety of tasks. To take a corporate example, one of the tasks of the meetings of a board of directors is to promulgate the business of the company. Shareholders meet to interact with company directors at the annual general meeting (AGM); experts meet to draft a report; an executive team meets to make major recommendations about the strategic direction of a company; employee involvement groups meet to solve problems in their workplace; project development teams meet to design a new product or service, or to provide input into the marketing strategy.

The type of meeting is dictated by its purpose. A shareholder meeting has several purposes. It is an opportunity for the directors to communicate with shareholders on any decisions taken on their behalf, and the outcomes of those decisions. It is also an opportunity for shareholders to hold their directors accountable. Stephen Mayne, the shareholder's advocate and activist, is well known for asking the difficult questions of directors, even travelling overseas to attend the News Corporation AGM. Individual shareholders may legitimately express dismay and anger at AGMs following the loss of value in what previously represented their future superannuation security, especially following information about some of the unscrupulous behaviour of directors before and during the global financial crisis (GFC) (remember Lehman Brothers in the US, and Storm Financial and Opes Prime in Australia). In meetings involving shareholders, it is incumbent upon the Chair to ensure that shareholders have an opportunity to voice their concerns, and to balance this with firm control, so that directors are also heard.

Governments and other social institutions, noted for their hierarchy and bureaucratic structures, usually hold formal meetings, which are scheduled annually in advance. The Chair chairs the meeting, by reason of the authority associated with the position. The 'speaker' in the parliament, or the president of a legislature, is the Chair facilitating government business, one of whose tasks is to ensure members of legislatures maintain a certain level of decorum (which is not always successfully accomplished). Governance structures in governments include not only the parliamentary or council meetings, but a host of statutory authorities and advisory committees. In government statutory authorities or industry advisory committees, the Chair is often appointed by Order of a Governor-in-Counsel, or the equivalent. This means that appointees, recommended by public service or other representative authorities, are given legal status by an official confirmation.

Not-for-profit and nongovernmental organisations (NGOs) depend on many volunteers for their workforce. They may be small sporting organisation, such as the local tennis or football club, or a large organisation, such as those with Olympic or other international connections. Alternatively, they can be service providers such as the Salvation Army or Red Cross, which manage large international aid operations, or small, local meals-on-wheels services for pensioners in their homes. As the context varies so do the responsibilities and roles of the members of the committees. In today's public service environment of public–private partnerships (PPPs) and service contracts, the Chair of a meeting of the management group might be required to ensure that staff are accountable for balancing budgets and expenditure. Likewise, he or she might need to balance the social needs and aspirations of the paid workforce with the values and expectations of the volunteers.

There is usually some person in authority who calls or authorises a meeting and acts as its Chair. That person's role and authority is influenced by whether he or she was elected or appointed the position, or assumed the authority from a formal position. In a not-for-profit organisation, if the Chair is also the major source of funds, his or her influence and opinions impact and shape the direction of the meeting.

Despite the influence of the contexts in which meetings are held, research confirms that there are ubiquitous recognised functions associated with meetings and processes that are evident in the progression of meetings and in the relationships and interactions between participants in meetings. The next section examines the contexts of different meetings and how to manage them, such as how to set the meeting dates, prepare for each meeting, and manage the agenda.

Preparing for a Meeting

Directors are busy people. They need advice about meetings to be included in their diaries well in advance of the dates of meetings. The annual calendar should be set out at the beginning of the year, and time conflicts resolved by the board secretary. The board calendar should include committee meetings that occur separately from full board meetings to ensure that all directors are aware of committee meeting times, and are available to attend.

Some good advice for the chairperson on preparing for an effective meeting is drawn from an article by Linda Nicholls, the Chair of the board of Australia Post (2006). Before each meeting, an effective Chair meets with the managing director or CEO and the board secretary to confirm the agenda and review the papers. Preparation includes determining the content, order and pace of the agenda, and the relevance of the papers.

Each agenda includes: reports on items from an annual work plan for the board; items from previous meetings; and new items brought forward by management. These are sorted into the priority in which they should be addressed:

- Items for decision;
- Items for discussion;
- Items for information; and
- Items for noting.

If the item is for decision, the decisions to be taken must be spelled out in a paper. At the start of the paper are the recommendations, set out in a form suitable for moving directly into the minutes.

The issues must be clearly identified in a paper. This need not be long. On major items, the CEO may prepare a one-page memo that outlines his or her proposal and the three main reasons why this makes sense, plus the things that caused the most concern to him or her in arriving at this recommendation. This helps focus director attention within the reading materials, and 'legitimises' debate and discussion without threatening the CEO's authority to come to such determinations (Beatty 2010).

If the issues are complex, the paper should include a one-page executive summary. So that the committee or board is clear about the discussion framework and the purpose of the paper, the key questions to be discussed will be presented at the beginning of the paper. What exactly is the meeting to discuss? Which two or three points are important? This helps management gain real input from the board on significant issues.

If an item is for noting, the paper must make clear what exactly is being noted – for example, that a project is on time and on budget, or that a new issue has arisen that may be relevant for the next meeting. If an item is for information, it is tabled at the meeting or circulated separately. It may be an attachment to the meeting papers, but should not be listed as an agenda item nor discussed.

A running sheet with a time set against each item has a number of benefits. It helps the Chair ensure that appropriate time is devoted to the important issues: that the board does not 'talk too much about the bicycle racks and race through the nuclear reactor decision'. The discipline of timing the agenda items can also highlight when a meeting is attempting too many matters in the time available, and whether some items, such as strategic planning, might not be more effectively addressed in a one or two day special planning session.

We have all attended meetings where the presenter will not get to the point. Some people enjoy talking and have difficulty presenting reports without going on too long. A good Chair sets a time limit, and advises the presenter of the time constraint before the meeting. This helps to encourage more succinct and targeted reporting. Yet another key task for the Chair is to assess the quality of the papers to be presented at the meeting. Poor papers are a major cause of committees and boards making poor decisions, or having difficulties reaching a decision (Beatty 2010).

Meeting Papers

The papers supporting each agenda item should be adequate and appropriate enough for the directors to reach a decision or have a meaningful discussion. Research into business communication suggests that, when communicating company information on an important company policy, oral communication that is followed by written communication is the most efficient, while communicating without written communication is the least efficient. In other words, a written paper is an important adjunct to an oral presentation.

Papers that are not right should be rewritten before the meeting or the item should be withdrawn. The Chair reviews the papers and raises any issues, concerns, gaps or areas for clarification in the papers, so that the executive making a report can be prepared to address these concerns at the meeting. The managing director or board secretary should then talk with the executive concerned. If one of the members has a special interest or expertise in an issue, that member should also be given the opportunity to review the relevant papers. Normally, a Chair would contact the member to obtain his or her views prior to the meeting.

There is a balance to be found between providing enough information so that members are fully informed, and swamping the members with hundreds of pages of text. The characteristics of members also factor into the appropriate page limit. Our experience is that business people typically do not want to be overloaded with unnecessary text. On the other hand, the more the weight of the paper, the more university board members feel comfortable. In reality, too much or too little should be a wakeup call for further investigation by members.

If members are to add value to the discussion of the issues, they should receive the papers at least a week before a meeting in order to allow them time to read, digest and think about the issues. The meeting is not the time to think about them for the first time. Nothing is more irritating to a Chair than to see a member, while the committee or board is discussing an item, trying to scan the next item because they are not prepared.

Committee and Board Dynamics

Corporate meetings entail a group of people with shared responsibilities and clear accountabilities strategising together, reaching decisions together and working together with management who plan and implement the decisions. According to best practice guidelines for well-functioning committees and boards, the members share a sense of team spirit, and work together to achieve a common objective which could not usually be accomplished by an individual (Bosch 1995). The Chair has two major tasks: achievement of the objectives or formal functions of a board or committee (which constitute the reasons for having a board or committee); and maintenance of the processes and interactions that achieve its informal functions (i.e. satisfaction of the individual needs for social interaction).

On executive teams, there may or may not be a permanent team leader or Chair. An individual may take the leadership role, or leadership may be shared by means of various individuals taking different roles at different stages of the team development or task achievement, or taking control at the stage in achievement of goals that demands their particular expertise.

An effective committee has some clear characteristics. Many are listed in Table 2.1 below.

Table 2.1. Characteristics of an effective board or committee meeting

Chairs are competent and have integrity
Members and leaders have high confidence and trust in each other
Members are loyal to one another and to the leader
Members support each other and learn together to develop the potential of individual
    members and the group
Members know when to conform and when not to, and for what purposes
Members communicate fully and frankly in dialogue and exchanges
Group values and goals match the needs of members and their organisation
Members exhibit integrity and maintain the confidentiality of group discussions

Newly appointed committees or groups often behave differently from those whose members have been together for longer periods of time. When members are first brought together as a whole, there is usually a period of learning, an induction period, where they become familiar with the strengths and weaknesses of the business and of each other. An understanding of how this develops can help to better manage the group, as well as better teach newly appointed individuals to perform as members of such groups.

Understanding the processes, or 'group dynamics', that take place in meetings is grounded in research into teams and groups. As a team develops, it goes through five stages: forming, storming, norming (or integrating), performing and adjourning (Tuckman 1965; Wood et al. 1998). When a group meets for the first time, the members and leaders get to know one another. At the forming stage, individuals begin to identify with other group members.

Their concerns may include: What can the group offer me? What will I be asked to contribute? What is acceptable role behaviour? What task does this group hope to accomplish? This forming stage is typically characterised by courtesy and politeness. The Chair's role is to anticipate and provide answers to such questions.

In the second stage, storming, members begin challenging each other. This may cause healthy conflict, tension or hostility to emerge. For example, conflict may emerge over leadership and authority. Yet through these struggles, individuals begin to understand each other's personal styles, and efforts begin towards clarifying goals and possible alternatives for action. Outside demands, including premature expectations for performance results, may create pressure at this time.

In the third stage, norming, the members become integrated as a team – moving beyond disagreements, resolving differences, and beginning the real work of working together. At this stage the members are investigating and establishing trust and group norms. Norms are the rules or standards about the behaviour that group members are expected to display. They establish the basic principles and rules that will determine the power, duties and rights of both the committee and its members.

Among committee norms are those regarding expected performance, attendance at meetings, punctuality, preparedness, respect for other members, etc. Norms give rise to expectations of acceptable behaviours and outcomes that, if met, facilitate high levels of contribution and achievement. The failure to meet norms can cause dissonance in members. When a member violates a norm, other members typically respond in ways that attempt to enforce the norm. The danger at this stage is that members may discourage minority views and tendencies to deviate from expected norms, exposing the group to the problem of 'group think', discussed later in this section. Another danger is that the enforcement of norms may consume a committee's time and energy; to prevent that from occurring, committees should establish a code of conduct, such as that described in the third part of this book.

Groups themselves will tend to apply negative sanctions to members whose behaviours are not compatible with group norms. Sherif and Sherif (2009) reported in their studies that sanctions were seen in forms of urging, insulting or cold-shouldering the offenders. The more significant the activity was to the identity and maintenance of the group, the greater the pressure to conform to the group norms. This applies especially to the leader of the group. The lessons for Chairs and members to take from this study are that these types of behaviours are common in groups, and that both categories of responses need to be managed if attendance at meetings is to be a satisfying experience.

Table 2.2. The Chair's role in managing group processes

Stage in group processes	Role of the Chair
Forming	Asserts purpose of meeting
	Defines mission and objectives
	Distributes information
	Develops support of vision, values and processes
Storming	Continues to clarify purpose of meetings, and mission and objectives
	Clarifies roles and responsibilities
	Limits personal attacks
	Resolves conflict
	Keeps meeting on track
	Keeps cheerful and confident
Norming	Exerts authority
	Keeps focus on purpose and tasks
	Supports and encourages participation; uses psychological reinforcement
	Supports development of group identity
	Summarises achievements
	Begins representation of the group to stakeholders
Performing	Focuses on the task
	Gives feedback on accomplishments and progress
	Encourages reports from members or subcommittees
	Facilitates making decisions on future actions

Performing occurs when the members work together to achieve the committee's objectives. This stage sees the emergence of a mature, organised and well-functioning group of members able to deal appropriately with complex tasks and internal disagreements. The members are motivated by group goals and are generally satisfied. Members of committees do not usually perform together at a high level from the start, yet every Chair hopes to reach this stage eventually, when members can take responsibility for the achievement of both the formal and informal functions described above.

A final stage is sometimes added, adjourning, when the team either moves to a new task or disperses. Wood et al. (1998) suggest that this is an especially important stage for task forces, committees and the like who may convene quickly and then disband: 'The willingness of members to disband when the job is done and to work well together in future responsibilities, group or otherwise, is an important long-run test of group success' (Wood et al. 1998, 305).

The Chair has different roles at each stage of the group development (Table 2.2). In the forming stage, the leader sets out the expectations of the members of the committee by providing information, setting objectives and modelling the desired behaviours.

By the second stage, storming, the Chair moves the group towards its task, and works at maintaining the members' interest and commitment. The Chair provides individual support for members; encourages participation and dialogue; acts as gatekeeper when some members want to dominate; indicates solidarity and warmth; encourages ideas; and summarises achievements. These responsibilities are part of the maintenance of the social system that enables the members to work effectively together and get their job done.

Providing feedback to the members is essential in the performing stage in order to encourage and support completion of the group tasks. Subcommittees should be formed and active, and their leaders should report to the full meeting. If the meeting is productive and successful, it is easier for the Chair and the members to maintain a positive climate and good relations, and to achieve their objectives. As the group moves forward, it should begin reaching decisions.

Communication

The very essence of meetings is communication. Without effective communication, the idea of a meeting would be nonsensical. Communication in meetings takes a number of different forms. There is the oral transfer of information – usually supported by papers, as discussed earlier in this section – as well as other techniques that facilitate communication.

In a well-managed meeting, members focussed on accomplishing their task of making decisions can be involved in a vigorous exchange, which involves sharing ideas and working through various beliefs, attitudes and options for decision making. Techniques that facilitate this exchange are dialogue, active listening and the use of silence. Here the influence of coalitions, with their different values, beliefs, information and preferences, comes into play. Conflict, as indicated above, can be both positive and negative. From a negative perspective, lack of trust and hidden agendas can lead to undesirable or ineffective outcomes. From a positive perspective, conflict challenges the status quo, stimulates interest and curiosity, and can produce new ideas and innovative resolutions to problems. How to handle difficult meetings is discussed in this section (Part Two).

Another form of communication is nonverbal communication. Meetings are conducted basically through the medium of speech, but that is not the only form of communication. We also convey powerful messages through our movements and gestures, which are dubbed 'nonverbal communication'. Nonverbal communication is a curious term in that it is one of the few which is negatively defined; it does not say what it is, but rather what it is not. If we were to try to be more precise, it would include movement (kinesics), physical distance (proximals), visuals (gaze, facial features and expressions, etc.) and touch (violent or caressing). Bull (2001) has given us an account which he subtitles 'on how our bodies can speak volumes'. Among the significant points he makes is that nonverbal communication is mostly used for emotional and interpersonal relationships. He noted that nonverbal communication is often so closely synchronised with speech that it is really an integral part of the process of communication (see also Hinde 1971).

One of the issues of which one must be aware is that this substantive field of nonverbal communication is not as clear as some writers would have their readers believe. There is no doubt that nonverbal communication is as important in relationships as other forms of communication – such as that of specific language, or of visual symbolic entities (e.g. national flags, religious symbols, and codified gestures such as salutes). What is not yet clear are which forms of nonverbal communication are universal across cultures, which are broadly specific (as in, say, European cultures), and which are stylised and recognisable only within specific cultures.

It is also beneficial to be aware of the substantial variations in nonverbal communication. This issue is related to Ardrey's (1966) concept of territoriality. As he has amply demonstrated, all higher species appear to be driven (amongst other things) by a territorial imperative. This phenomenon is widely evident in human behaviour in diverse situations. It holds that we constantly define our territory and resent what we perceive to be incursions. For example, someone who stands close and waves his or her arms in your face is invading your personal space. A social instance is that of marking out a space on the beach, putting out your towel and then finding people walking on it.

Nonverbal communication can also be conveyed by things not done. The failure to send a note of thanks for some extraordinary service; the omission of engaging in occasional eye contact in interpersonal conversations; and the failure to say constructive and complimentary things when the occasion calls, are all examples. All that we can clearly conclude is the importance of such communication, and the need to be wary of being too confident that we know the meanings of kinesics, proximals, visuals and touch.

Dialogue

An alternative approach is 'dialogue', which literally means a conversation between two or more persons. 'Dialogue' comes from the Greek noun 'dialectic': the art of critical examination into the truth of an opinion, a process of thought by which mutually contradictory principles are seen to merge in a higher truth which comprehends them (Adair 1984). Dialogue is described as the discipline that involves the capacity of a group or team to suspend assumptions and enter into a genuine 'thinking together' (Senge 1995). Senge distinguished between dialogue and discussion. In discussion, different views are presented and defended, and there is a search for the best views to support decisions that must be made. In contrast, dialogue supports the creative exploration of complex and subtle issues, which involves a suspension of one's own views and a deep 'listening' to one another. The table below gives some elements.

Perhaps most decisions can be reached fairly readily by discussion; but what approach is appropriate in the face of a real impending crisis? Dialogue can challenge our 'mental models': our previously held views and beliefs about our world. It brings the different perspectives of members together to explore complex and difficult issues from many points of view. When people suspend their own assumptions, they can observe and assess their own thinking as well as that of others. This process goes beyond what is normally thought of as 'thinking' and allows people to 'participate in a pool of common meaning' (Senge 1995, 242). It helps guide and shape our perceptions and can produce consequences that, as individuals, we do not really want. The three basic conditions that Senge proposes are necessary for dialogue are:

- That all participants 'suspend' their assumptions, literally hold them 'as if suspended before us', accessible to questioning and observation;
- That all participants regard one another as colleagues;
- That there be a 'facilitator' who 'holds the context' of dialogue.

Suspending our assumptions about what we believe is right is threatening. Equally, we may feel compelled to keep quiet when our views conflict with the majority-held beliefs. We may disagree about the reality of performance targets, the influence of community groups opposed to a development, the safety of working conditions, or some other issue requiring committee action. People will only disclose their fears if they feel 'safe': that is; if they trust and have confidence in the integrity of the other members of their committee. Being a colleague does not mean that you have to agree or share the same views, However, if there is no trust, then members will engage in defensive routines.

Dialogue does not mean that there is an absence of conflict but, rather, that the conflict is appropriately managed. Members are supported when they speak up, and encouraged to give up defensive routines used to protect themselves from embarrassment that comes from exposing one's thinking.

Senge (1995) has given several examples of where defensive behaviour leads to poor decisions in organisations. Among them are: responding with 'that's an interesting idea' when we have no intention of taking the idea seriously, or when we want to avoid having to consider it; and believing, as brilliant and forceful leaders, that we know all the answers, such that no one else feels able to give another opinion (recent examples of heads of government come to mind). Here the leader's forcefulness may be a defence against questioning his or her ideas.

It needs to be said that the Chair who acts as a facilitator has a difficult task. That Chair must keep the process moving and the discussion under control, but at the same time ensure that the participants 'own' the discussion. This requires a fine sense of balance between encouraging the flow of ideas and ensuring that a decision is reached. If the Chair is used to having his or her views dominate, or if junior members of a committee withhold their views through fear, then dialogue will not work and ideas for creative decision making will be lost. Schein (1995 quoted in Wood et al. 1998, 311) observed that groups may make decisions through any of the six following methods:

- Lack of response – a course of action is chosen by default or lack of interest;
- Authority rule – one person dominates and determines the course of action;
- Minority rule – a small subgroup dominates and determines the course of action;
- Majority rule – a vote is taken to choose among alternative courses of action;
- Consensus – not everyone wants to pursue the same course of action, but everyone agrees to give it a try;
- Unanimity – everyone in the group wants to pursue the same course of action.

As noted above in the discussion of formal decision making, a common way or reaching a decision is by majority rule. This means of reaching a decision parallels the democratic political system but may cause problems associated with the outcomes of the decision. The process of voting can create 'winners' and 'losers'. The losers may feel left out or discarded without having a fair say and, as a result, feel less committed to implementing the actions required by the decision.

The decision by unanimity is when all members agree totally on the course of action to be taken. The decision by consensus, on the other hand, is when not all members completely agree on the course of action, but are willing to go along with the decision. When a consensus is reached, even those who may oppose the chosen course of action know that they have been listened to and have had a fair chance to influence the decision outcome.

Table 2.3. Reaching consensus

Try to get the underlying assumptions regarding the issues out into the open where
they can be discussed.

Listen to (and pay attention to) what others have to say. Effective listening is the most
distinguishing characteristic of successful groups.

Be cautious of early, quick, easy agreements and compromises. They are often based
on erroneous assumptions that need to be challenged.

Avoid competing and arguing. With those behaviours, either the group wins or no
one wins.

Try to avoid getting the meeting to vote in a manner that splits the group into
'winners' and 'losers'. Such an approach also encourages either/or thinking when
there may be other ways, and it fosters argument rather than rational discussion.

Encourage others to contribute their ideas; the group needs all the information it has
available.

Discussion is what is required to reach decisions about projects on which
there is general agreement among members. Dialogue is most suitable for the
exploration of complex issues, i.e. when there is likely to be a wide divergent
of views, or when not all members have the level of information required
to reach an informed decision. Open dialogue can help all members learn
about an issue and reach some consensus. After the issues have been explored,
the Chair presents and weighs the alternative views, summarises the common
view, and moves to discussing and then reaching a decision.

Active Listening

Active listening is seen as a basic component of dialogue. There are two sides
to communicating a message: sending the message and receiving the message,
or 'listening'. To fully listen means to pay close attention to what is being said
beneath the words. You listen not only to the 'music', but to the very essence
of the person speaking. You listen not only for what someone knows, but for
'who he or she is' (Isaacs 1996).

Active listening is contrasted with passive listening. Active listening is a
technique that gives feedback to the speaker, with the purposes of helping the
speaker say what he or she means, confirming the message, and, through reflection,
doing the work that adds to an understanding of the deep structure in the language.
The following guidelines are useful in this regard (Wood et al. 1998, 566):

- Listen for message content: try to hear exactly what the source is saying in
  the message.
- Listen for feelings: try to identify how the source feels in terms of the message
  content. Is the message pleasing or displeasing to the source? Why?

- Respond to feelings: let the source know that you recognise his or her feelings as well as the message content.
- Note all cues, both verbal and nonverbal: be sensitive to nonverbal communication as well as verbal communication. Identify mixed messages that need to be clarified.
- Reflect back to the source, in your own words, what you think you are hearing: paraphrase and restate the verbal and nonverbal messages as feedback to which the source can respond with further information.

Silence and Speech

There are things to refrain from doing. Among them is the constant use of speech. It is relatively rare to enforce silence, although that is sometimes necessary in order to prevent an overtalker from dominating the meeting.

Silence finds itself on a number of ceremonial occasions: the two minutes silence to honour the dead, the right to silence in court (and thus protection from self-incrimination), the powerful effects of boycotting, and the values placed by some religious orders on a vow of silence.

Such silence can provide an opportunity for reflection, and for allowing tempers to cool. Silence can also be effectively used to make a point. One might, for example look at a speaker and say nothing; when a group of listeners do so, the disapproval is palpable.

Nonverbal Behaviour and Body Language

Everyone uses nonverbal communication. Interest in nonverbal communication grew in the 1960s following the wide range of research conducted by Michael Argyle (see Argyle 1988), and is described for the general reader in a number of books (see, for example, Pease 1997). For the most part, nonverbal communication is involuntary and probably inherent. Although there are cultural differences, most of the basic nonverbal communication gestures are the same all over the world. People smile when they are happy and frown when sad or angry. In business transactions, nodding means yes and shaking the head from side to side means no. Open palms are a message that the person is open and honest. However, if a policeman holds up his palm, every nationality knows it means 'stop'. Both giving and reading non-verbal messages can be learned.

Being skilled in reading nonverbal cues means not only recognising individual gestures, but also being aware that interpreting their meaning usually involves analysing a cluster of cues.

A simple cue such as crossing arms may be a defensive or a negative pose, and is an indication for the Chair to change his or her behaviour. A person flushing

Table 2.4. Nonverbal cues and their meanings

Nonverbal behaviour	Meaning
Smile	Happy
Frown	Sad or angry
Nod head	Yes
Shake head	No
Shrugging shoulders	I do not understand what you mean
Staring	A compliment in Italy An offence in Australia
Crossed arms and/or legs	A defensive pose or a negative attitude
Crossed arms or legs with a clenched fist and red face	Attack is imminent!
Chin down	Hostility: I don't believe what you are saying; or, I disagree with you
Hand covering the mouth or part of the mouth and/or Facial muscle twitching Contracting of pupils Sweating at the brow Flushing Increased eye blinking Rubbing their eye with a finger Pulling at their collar	The person speaking is telling a lie
Hand covering mouth and thumb is pressed against the cheek	If a person does this while you are speaking: you are telling a lie
Stroking the chin	The person is evaluating what you say, or has made a decision
Palms are up and arms open	Indicates honesty
Palms are up	Submissive and nonthreatening
Palms down	Indicates authority
Palms rubbed together	Indicates enthusiasm (or may be cold!)
Head resting on hand	Bored
Index finger points up and thumb under chin	Negative thoughts
Pen or finger in the mouth	Unsure

Source: Pease (1997).

may be excited or simply hot, or may have too tight a collar. On the other hand, if a person is delivering a report on performance figures and feels that he or she is not telling the whole truth or hiding something, that person is likely to exhibit a cluster of cues: hand touching the mouth, face muscle twitching, pupils contracting, flushing, and increased eye blinking. The perceptive member will know to ask some penetrating questions. Interpretation also needs to take into account the context in which the behaviour occurs. Some of the nonverbal cues that are relevant to meetings are listed in Table 2.4.

There are many more. We have to recognise that there are some general patterns of nonverbal communication that are universal; there are, however, others that are culturally stylised. We need to be sensitive to how valuable it is to observe nonverbal communication and, at the same time, be prepared to recognise that we may be mistaken in particular instances.

If, while speaking, a Chair sees members with their heads resting on their hands, those members may be tired, but they may also be bored. If the same members are sitting up with a hand touching their cheek but not supporting their head, they are showing interest in what is being said. Alternatively, if they place a thumb under their chin and an index finger points upwards, then they are thinking negatively about your message. A few minutes later when they rub their chins, they have reached a decision.

One of the seminal works on the expression of emotions in animals and men (and thus attitudes) is that of Darwin. For a reprint see Darwin (1998), and an update on that work by Russell and Fernandez-Dols (1997). The use of such expressions to detect lying is available in the work of Ekman (1985). General behavioural taboos are to be found in the work of Axtell (1998 and 1999) – and also Sherif and Sherif (2009). The general approach to understanding cultural precepts and communication may be found in Mantovani (2000), Marx (2001), and Wharton (2009).

Territory and Personal Space

Research shows that meetings can be influenced by the location in which a meeting is held, and by the seating positions of the members (Argyle 1988). If the meeting is to resolve a contentious issue between two people, then a meeting held in the office of one of them will give that person an advantage, because the meeting will be held on that person's 'territory'.

Each person has his or her own personal space. This space goes wherever the person goes. Territory extends to include the areas that exist around possessions, such as one's home, car, personal chair or office. Once people have selected their seats at a first meeting, many will return to the same seat on following occasions (which is one of the aids for Chairs trying to recall the names of members!). The amount of personal space differs in different contexts and in different cultures. The area of personal space in English-speaking cultures is generally similar. It can be broken into four zones:

- Intimate zone (15–45 cms / 6–18 inches);
- Personal zone (46 cms–1.22 metres / 18–48 inches);

- Social zone (1.2–3.6 metres / 4–12 feet); and
- Public zone (over 3.6 metres / 12 feet).

Only those who are emotionally close are allowed to enter the intimate zone, i.e. lovers, parents, children and close personal friends. This zone is smaller or bigger in other cultures. There are many stories about Japanese or Arab people who step forward to close the gap with a person to whom they are speaking, only to find their companion backing away. As Japanese step forward to adjust their space, people who come from less crowded and low contact societies, such as Australians, keep stepping backwards to maintain their space. This can move both parties right across a room. In one study of Japanese and Americans, the Americans tended to describe the Japanese as 'pushing' and 'familiar', while the Japanese interpreted the American behaviour as 'cold' and 'stand-offish' (Pease 1997, 25).

There is a host of unwritten rules to safeguard ourselves in public spaces. Think how people react to crowding at concerts or in elevators, or sitting next to someone on an aircraft. Among the rules are: you do not speak to your neighbour; you avoid eye contact; you do not show any emotion; you face the door in elevators.

Ownership of territory in meetings is also related to public space. When a person claims a seat at a meeting, it is unlikely that another will take that seat. Much of the research into seating has taken place in offices. There are four basic positions:

- The corner position: people usually sit around the corner of a desk to avoid territorial ownership, which occurs when people sit opposite each other across a meeting or on opposite sides of a desk. The partial presence of the desk produces a partial barrier and provides protections for the owner.
- The cooperative position: here people sit side by side. It is common when people think the same or work together on a project.
- The competitive position: people sit opposite one another across a desk or table.
- The independent position: people working in a library or visiting a restaurant may wish to be alone.

This research has some implications for meetings. In order to avoid the 'competitive position', meeting tables are usually oval. This has the advantage of sitting people next to each other and avoiding power plays. Being seated higher than other members, as, for example, a judge in a court, is a sign of position and power. Chairs also hold power that is indicated by their position at the table. Usually, a Chair assumes a position of authority and sits at the head of the table, usually facing the door. This is because it is the seat surveying the room and indicating the most power. It has the advantage of being able to see all the members, and keep an eye on any latecomers.

A well-prepared Chair may also have designated seating for members. Those who support the Chair sit beside him, forming a power block, or sit opposite so that the competitive position is taken by a supporter. Opponents who might gang up against the Chair are separated so that it is more difficult to act in unison. If there are two members who are regularly aggressive in conflict, they are seated so that they are not directly facing each other across the table in a competitive position.

Behaviour in Meetings

Meetings are used in order to harness the collective wisdom and expertise of the participants. The pitfalls to meetings have their origins in human limitations and poor procedures. The latter has been addressed in Part One of this book. This section addresses some of the difficulties that emerge from human weaknesses or limitations, and some of the disruptive strategies that have been used in previous meetings. Knowing about them enables the effective Chair or member to recognise them and intervene in a timely manner so that the business and experienced satisfaction of meetings is not inhibited.

Research into satisfied and dissatisfied groups shows that the profiles of members of satisfied groups exhibit higher numbers of suggestions, more often followed by positive reactions and less often by negative reactions and disagreement, than satisfied groups.

The positive responses in Table 2.5 are the types of responses that might be proactively practiced by members who seek to promote the informal functions of groups. Behaviours expected of successful members include respecting

Table 2.5. Responses by members to new ideas

Positive responses	Negative responses
Shows solidarity	Disagrees
Raises others' status	Shows passive rejection
Gives help – rewards	Shows formality
Gives suggestions, direction	Withholds help
Gives opinion, evaluation, analysis: expresses feelings	Shows tension
Asks for suggestions, direction, possible ways of action	Shows antagonism
Gives orientation and information: repeats, clarifies and confirms	Deflates others' status
	Defends or asserts self

Table 2.6. Qualities and behaviours of difficult members

- A history of being a nuisance, and evidence of a disturbed personal life (e.g. drinking problems, pathological jealousy, sexual incompetence, lack of social skills – or any combination of these).
- A belief in being right, without reference to outside experts (the mark of the passionate ideologue). Assuming self-perceived views are right simply because of holding them.
- Presenting a one-sided view of an issue (e.g. listing a string of concerns without a balance of presenting what else was done in the action that might counterbalance those concerns: omitting facts and counterfacts, argument and counterargument, and a balanced conclusion).
- Pursuing a person rather than a principle, and continuing to harass the person and complain about the person rather than work constructively toward a solution. Arguing *ad hominem* against the person making the argument rather than arguing the substance of the argument.
- Not attempting to resolve an ethical issue by a collegial approach. Going behind a colleague's back to lobby, complain, or improperly intervene.
- When shown to be wrong, never offering an apology.

---

others, partaking in teamwork, trusting others and maintaining confidentiality. Successful members work with others by giving their suggestions, contributing to decisions and helping others. On the other hand, Table 2.5 also shows the types of behaviours that are reactive and not supportive: disagreeing, and being aggressive, antagonistic, tense and withdrawn.

When a member engages in a particular type of response, it appears that the response is a reflection of that member's psychological profile. Hence, that member is more likely to continue this type of response in further interactions (Table 2.6). A perceptive Chair will recognise a member's usual mode of operation and be ready to respond. A perceptive member will identify his or her usual response, and become aware of how it may be perceived by other group members.

Other difficulties in meetings can emerge because of a particular mindset or an individual attribute, such as personality – or because of group perceptions, which colour how information and events are processed.

Mindset of Members

The concepts of mindset and culture have been addressed by many researchers and writers. A human mind seems to be programmed by culture to perceive and respond to the world in certain ways. The result is what we hold to be a set way of 'understanding' (Senge's mental models) and reasoning, which leads to an evaluation of events, and provides the basis on which decisions are made. Such mindsets influence international political relations; development assistance policies and their implementation; and conduct of international and business affairs. One might also say that such mindsets have a powerful impact on the progression of committee debates. An example of a personal mindset is that of someone who has a conspiratorial view of the world, being disposed to see conspiracies in objectively innocuous events.

One may be aware of mindsets among committee members. Committee member mindsets may be allied to the notion of 'delegate' or 'representative'. Committee members are appointed to attend to the needs of the organisation to which they are appointed, and to make decisions for the good of that organisation: not to pursue the interests of the organisation for which they are delegates.

Committee Membership and Personality

There is the problem that some aggressive personalities may come to dominate the debate in meetings, but that is one of the prices that we have to pay for such social enterprises. It is argued here that such a problem is a preferable risk to that of not having such debates and methods of resolution. As Waldron (1999) notes, debate is certainly preferable to the system of legislation, for example, where bills are thrust into force by numbers rather than by necessarily reasoned debate amongst all members. Further, this work argues that such dominance may be substantially diminished by prior agreement about the rules of debate.

We need to be mindful that the majority of honest committee members may suffer as a result of what they say, or support, or vote against, at the hands of the vociferous few. The reality is that, right or wrong, such members may be seen as nuisances, social incompetents, or time-wasting influences. We do not know how many are motivated by just and professional concerns or how many are malicious, pathologically jealous, psychiatrically disturbed, or just plain nuisances.

The notion that there are psychopaths abroad in corporations was examined by Clark (2005). His work denotes the kind of problems that can and do arise, and canvasses some of the ways to recognise those problems, and to deal with them. In particular, he exercises caution about the corporate psychopath whose actions are disturbing, socially dysfunctional, and not in the best corporate interests. The extreme psychopath is one problem, and a most serious one. Additionally, there is the problem of the member misfit, who can range from being the commonplace advocate of unpopular causes (and thus performing a valuable function), to someone who is a destructive nuisance.

We note some pertinent cues (Table 2.7) to help identify such a person, and to help decide which type of misfit best describes him or her.

Relationships between the CEO and the Chair

The relationship between the Chair and the chief executive officer (CEO) is critical to the performance of an organisation. At its best, the relationship between the Chair and the CEO is built on mutual respect and trust; 'At worst, it's an ongoing battle for power and control' (Stuart 2008, 32). The successful performances of each depend on this relationship, and some potential areas of conflict can be avoided by having clear statements of their roles, duties and responsibilities, on which the appointees sign off when taking up their offices.

In theory, the Chair and the committee or board set the direction for the organisation, while the CEO implements and manages the strategy. In practice, establishing the strategic mission and objectives of a company is an interactive exchange between the CEO and the committee or board that results in agreement on what has to be done. There is a general consensus in large companies that Chairs and committees or boards do not interfere in the management of a company. This does not apply to owner/manager companies found in families and small businesses. Thus a balance needs to be maintained between being friendly and still being able to stand back and address serious performance problems. One such way of avoiding such problems is to require regular reports of performance indicators to the meetings, such as employment turnover, employee culture surveys, or community engagement.

The Chair is often a sounding board for the CEO, and also a possible mentor. At the same time, the Chair is responsible for assessing the CEO's performance, and for CEO selection and dismissal. Firing a CEO can have serious ramifications for an organisation's reputation (and share price if it is a commercial organisation). This applies especially to CEOs that were the initial entrepreneurs in their organisations, and thus reluctant to leave. A good long-term succession plan can help to manage the transition. If there are difficulties with the performance of the CEO, the committee or board may need to meet *in camera*, without the presence of any internal directors, in an external location where a response can be worked out in private. The Chair and members may need to ask the right questions at such meetings. These may take several forms:

- Open ended to clarify the problem: How, and in what way, will this problem impact the business?
- Closed: From the perspective of meeting performance targets, should the CEO be dismissed?

- Direct: From a PR perspective, how should we proceed?
- Relay: How do the rest of you feel about that?
- Consensus: Am I correct in saying that we have reached consensus on going ahead with the dismissal of the CEO?

Other problems can also arise. As Grady (quoted in Stuart 2008) noted in a commercial context: 'The CEO on the other hand, is the source of all information about the company. Sometimes meetings do not have any idea about what is really going on because all the information they're getting is screened by the CEO'. The CEO may withhold information from a meeting, or cover up anything that appears as a personal threat. In such cases, members of the meeting need to become more informed by asking for briefings from both internal and external experts.

Chairs can also underperform, or be obliged to leave, because of difficult circumstances. Featherstone (2010) found that one in five CEOs left their positions during the 2008 global financial crisis, but few Chairs were forced to leave. He suggests that this may be because many Chairs performed well, or that underperforming Chairs may still be running their companies because their committees or boards had neither the processes nor the wills to make them perform. Without due process, and with many members nominated to their positions by the Chair, a meeting may be reluctant to address the problem.

In listed companies, shareholders elect the directors, and the directors elect the Chair. This means that a Chair who is forced out of his or her position can remain as a member. There is an erroneous assumption that any director may take on the position of Chair, but such is not the case because the Chair requires a particular mix of skills.

A dismissal of either members or the Chair should be based on the assessment of performance. A problem here is that, in many organisations, the Chair usually conducts the review, oversees the process, and controls the communication of results. For this reason, it is often desirable to have an independent review of the performances of the Chair, the meeting, and individual members by someone external to the organisation.

Hidden Agendas

Behaviours that could indicate hidden agendas (Table 2.7) include personal attacks, blaming and scapegoating tactics, complaining and grumbling behaviour, emotional outbursts and withdrawal into silence and sullenness (Argyris 1999).

Table 2.7. Evidence of hidden agendas

Personal attacks
Blaming and scapegoating
Complaining and grumbling
Emotional outbursts
Withdrawal into silence and sullenness
Interrupting others and refusing to listen
Failing to carry out agreements
Ambivalence of commitment or opinion
Divisiveness and forming factions

Source: Argyris (1999).

Groupthink

An important aspect of group interaction is that the 'whole is greater than the sum of the parts'. The means that the combined efforts of members can add value to the performance of the group in decision making. Hence, one purpose of holding a meeting is to facilitate active contributions of members to the shared activity. However, group decision making has its own problems.

Table 2.8. Indicators of 'groupthink'

Illusions of group invulnerability	Members believe the group is beyond criticism or attack
Collective rationalising of unpleasant data	Members refuse to accept or thoroughly consider contradictory data
Belief in inherent group morality	Members believe the group is 'right' and above reproach by outsiders
Negative stereotyping of outsiders	Members refuse to look realistically at other groups: they may view competitors as weak, evil or stupid
Pressure on dissenters	Members refuse to tolerate anyone who suggests that the group may be wrong; every attempt is made to get conformity to group wishes
Self-censorship	Members are unwilling to communicate personal concerns or alternative points of view to the group
Illusions of unanimity	Members are quick to accept consensus; they do so prematurely without testing its completeness
Self-appointed mind guards	Members of the group keep outsiders away and try to protect the group from hearing disturbing ideas or viewpoints

Source: Janis and Mann (1977).

Where all think alike, the term 'groupthink' has been coined. Groupthink occurs in highly cohesive groups when, due to a combination of factors, poor and often disastrous decisions are made. It was described by Janis (1972) following his study of the US executives' decision to invade Cuba. In that case, the president's team had high cohesiveness and was insulated from other sources of information. Individual members of the president's team did not want to disagree with the president and later reported that they thought that other members of the team were in agreement, and that perhaps they were the only one who had any doubts about the course to be taken. Without any evidence, they agreed that Cuba was evil and could not stand up to them. The cohesiveness removed any opportunities for rational discussion or disagreement, and resulted in the decision to invade, subsequently a poor decision. The factors involved in groupthink are given in Table 2.8.

Poor decision making is reinforced in leaders when they receive social support from the other committee or board members who concur with their judgements. Instead of using rational risk assessment models, the leader may be immersed in defensive avoidance tendencies.

Playing the Rules

The writers have seen cases where a committee member is aware of the rules, and plays them to dubious advantage. For example, a meeting that is only just quorate debates a motion and takes a straw poll. It then seems like the meeting may reject the motion that a member dearly wants to pass. That member may then get up to leave the meeting and say to the Chair 'Sorry Mr Chairman but I have to leave, and must point out that my going will leave the meeting without a quorum, and thus it cannot pass the motion'. This may be only a delaying tactic, but can give the dissenter time to mobilise support.

Corruption and Whistleblowing

Transparency International has the basic principle that corruption flourishes in secrecy, and thus that transparency is a fundamental principle. However, if a proposed new idea is that potential whistleblowers receive counselling before blowing the whistle, is that consistent with the preservation of privacy? Further, there is a possible indignity in assuming that there is a problem with the whistleblower that requires attention. It is by stating the investing values that any inquiry can exercise the human judgement that invariably accompanies dilemma resolution. One of the hardcore facts of the world is that there is more than one way of retribution for dissenters. The notion that whistleblowers can receive effective protection is not realistic. One is aware of the myriad ways that whistleblowers can be sanctioned, and well beyond the reach of legal redress.

This work is not about whistleblowing, but does alert the reader to be mindful of the implications of whistleblowing. For anyone contemplating blowing the whistle, there is some elementary advice worth considering. Among the questions one asks oneself are:

- Is it objectively a problem, or am I just finding the situation disagreeable?
- What does my family think?
- If it is a problem, have I gone through the proper channels to find a solution (or are the channels the problem)?
- Have I gotten professional legal advice?
- Do I have the documentation to support my concern? (Get it before you blow the whistle, because you won't get it afterwards.)
- Am I prepared to persist in my plaint?

Such questions are helpful in deciding action or nonaction. Blowing the whistle is not an action to be taken lightly, and thus preliminary steps should be considered. There are a host of websites designed to help the potential whistleblower, and they should be consulted.

Lack of Attendance at Meetings

As noted in the formal rules for meetings in this book, a quorum is required in order for a meeting to be legally constituted. If a person cannot attend, the Chair should be notified prior to the meeting. Lack of attendance at meetings is a problem because the aims and objectives of the meeting, plus the social maintenance tasks, cannot be accomplished if people do not participate. A minimum level of attendance is required if people are to function effectively together. Further, when a number of members are not present, the decisions may be biased in favour of a particular group.

The reasons for a member's nonattendance of a meeting may be genuine. In today's world, so many people are travelling on business that it is common to find half the members out of the country. In such cases it is likely that a member can gain access to a telephone and can be linked via teleconference or videoconference. Alternatively, as noted in the formal rules, one can appoint a proxy. Attendance at board meetings is disclosed in the Annual Reports. A Chair is responsible for counselling, or calling for dismissal of, a board member who has no relevant reason for not being present.

Assessment of Member and Committee or Board Performance

Evaluation of the committee or board, and of individual performance, is now used widely in both the private and public sectors. Used less often is the assessment of a Chair's performance, unless there is a crisis. Potential benefits, which the organisation, the meeting, and the individual directors accrue, are improved leadership and decision making, clarity of roles and duties, teamwork, and accountability (Kiel and Nicholson 2003). Evaluation of performance can also help meetings operate more efficiently, reduce risks, enhance reputations of members and their organisations, and provide protection to members in the face of legal challenges. Evaluation of directors is also an opportunity to ensure that the competency profile of the directors continues to meet the needs of the organisation.

This further reform is in keeping with the introduction of performance management at all levels. Performance management requires the setting of objectives and the assessment of performance against the objectives. It operates at a strategic level for institutions as a whole, and has been introduced at lower levels to measure the performance of business units, and both general and academic staff. It is important to ensure that every member has an opportunity to contribute. The Chair should monitor both the committee or board, and individual members' performances, recognising and praising those who made particularly relevant contributions, and counselling those who are too quiet or wasting the time of the meeting. Feedback closely following behaviour is the most effective and private counselling of poor performance, and is more effective than public criticism at meetings.

There are a number of frameworks against which committees or boards can assess their performance. Among the most well known that apply directly to board performance are the NACD's 'Report of the Blue Ribbon Commission on Director Professionalism' (National Association of Corporate Directors 2001); Carver's (1997) Policy Governance Model; the Standards Australia Governance Standards (2003); Kiel-Chisholm and Nicholson's compliance toolkit for assessing compliance with the ASX Corporate Governance Council's Principles (Kiel and Kiel-Chisholm et al. 2004); Leblanc and Gillies' (2005) review of meeting effectiveness; and, specifically relevant to universities, the National Governance Protocols for Higher Education Providers.

The private sector models are cognizant of the need for committees and boards to add value to their companies. Different additional issues are addressed in various models. Carver's model has an emphasis on board–management relationships, and Kiel and Nicholson's includes 'director protection', which, together with continuous improvement, is achieved through appropriate access to information and meeting papers, and insurance. Based on these and other board research, Armstrong (2004) and Armstrong and Unger (2009) developed an instrument for assessing committee or board performance, which addresses various items grouped under the headings:

- Leadership
- Structures and relationships
- Accountability and reporting
- Compliance with legal and governance requirements
- Performance in terms of tasks and informal performance
- Meetings and their procedures and management

This instrument lends itself to self-assessment, which has the advantages of, first, meeting the confidentiality requirements of committees and boards, and second, assuring the objective of self-assessment is continuous improvement. Whether a board or committee should engage in self-assessment – led by a Chair, or perhaps a member with HR experience, or by an external person – is a matter for the meeting. The importance of assessment is that it provides feedback to members on their performances, benchmarks for the board, and important motivation for the members.

Conclusion

The above discussion contains advice and insights, for both Chairs and members, on how a successful meeting should be managed. Much of it has focussed on the role of the Chair. However, in today's environment, there are a number of reasons why the members are as important as the Chair. First, gone are the days when members of committees or boards could simply come along for a good time with their friends. The legal liabilities of formally constituted boards and committees, who make decisions on behalf of their organisations, are real and shared by every individual committee and board member.

Second, the decisions addressed by committees are much more complex than they were only a few years ago, and much more diverse. Committees and boards (and executive committees), even in small companies, face not only financial performance targets for their companies, but may also be engaged in decisions about environmental pressures, human resources issues (such as occupational health and safety), marketing, corporate social responsibility, and community engagement. It is impossible for everyone to be an expert in each of these areas, but it is possible to obtain expert information and advice that will enable members to make informed decisions.

The selection of members, for example, is increasingly dictated by the types of competencies and other skills required for the particular positions that will contribute to company performance (Wan Yussoff and Armstrong 2010). The people who chair, or are members attending meetings in organisations, are therefore highly qualified for their positions. They will not wish to risk their reputations and waste their time in meetings that do not allow them the opportunity to contribute to decisions made in the name of their committee.

Related to this is the role of Chair; because of the complexity of the issues being faced, Chairs cannot act alone. They need the expertise of the members of their committees. A good Chair has a wealth of talent to call upon, and makes use of it. He or she facilitates the processes and manages the meeting such that the members participate in the discussions and contribute to the decisions. Should Chairs find themselves in a situation where members are not contributing, it may indicate that the time has come to pass the leadership onto another. Alternatively, it might be time to change the members!

Part Three

ETHICS

Introduction

In order for any meeting, or any organisation, to function well, it must function according to agreed standards and values. It is recognised that meetings are made effective by adherence to certain rules that comply with the values espoused by the organisation. For that reason, the attached code below provides a point of departure, which others may use to their advantage. It is not suggested that this is a totally inclusive code, or one that is universally accepted. It does, however, provide a frame of reference from which any new code can be developed. (See also Francis 1999, 2009; Francis and Mishra 2009.)

The primary advantages of ethics codes are that they can clarify our thoughts on what constitutes unethical behaviour; help professionals to think about ethical issues before they are confronted with the realities of the situation; provide employees with the opportunity to refuse to comply with unethical action; define the limits of what constitutes acceptable or unacceptable behaviour; and provide a mechanism for communicating professional ethics policy. Commitment to a code requires seven aspects, which are:

1. Having and knowing the ethics code;
2. Knowing the applicability of state and federal laws and regulations;
3. Knowing the rules and regulations of the institution where the employee works;
4. Engaging in continuing education in ethics;
5. Identifying when there is a potential ethical problem;
6. Learning a method of analysing ethical obligations in often complex situations; and
7. Consulting professionals knowledgeable about ethics.

Committee Charter

Every ethics committee needs a charter. The point of such a document is to set out the powers and responsibilities of the committee. In doing so, the charter also makes clear the reach and scope of its functions. A charter sets out clearly what is – and, by implication, what is not – within its power.

Additional features of the charter include:

- How the committee is constituted (how many members, and how they are appointed);
- How long each member serves, and how members are replaced;
- Rules for the conduct of meetings, including for how frequently meetings are to be held;
- To whom the committee is responsible;
- To what extent the confidentiality of complaints is maintained, and what is not to be confidential.

Reporting

An organisation that has a code and an ethics committee should not be content to leave it at that. Accountability is an integral part of the ethical infrastructure. When reporting on what the ethics committee has done, it is customary to present the statistics of the cases (41 complaints, 3 criminal charges, 24 resolved by negotiation, etc.). It is rarely necessary to record the details, or the identities of those involved, to the parent body. Indeed, a disposition too ready to reveal identities is a significant deterrent to those who would otherwise use the ethics committee to resolve disputes. There are clearly exceptions to this, such as cases in which expulsion from employment is involved, or where deregistration is recommended. The balance to be maintained here is between raising the status of the ethics committee to one that is trusted and used properly, and keeping that committee accountable to another responsible body.

Codes of Ethics

Codes of ethics may be disseminated through company booklets, annual reports and induction, and training programs. The primary advantages of ethics codes are that they:

- Clarify management's thoughts on what constitutes unethical behaviour;
- Help employees to think about ethical issues before they are confronted with the realities of the situation;
- Provide employees with the opportunity to refuse to comply with unethical action;
- Define the limits of what constitutes acceptable and unacceptable behaviour; and
- Provide a mechanism for communicating managerial policy.

Clearly a code of ethics is the most visible sign of an organisation's philosophy in the realm of ethical behaviour. In order to be meaningful, it must assist in the induction and training of employees; truly state its basic principles and expectations; and realistically focus on potentially ethical dilemmas (Francis 2000).

The primacy of responsibility lies at the heart of ethics. The important question is, do our responsibilities lie primarily with our conscience, with the company, with business, or with the community at large? Professional and business mobility work against developing loyalty to one company, and may generate a disposition to self-loyalty. Thus it is recommended that:

- A clear code of business ethics be set up, printed, and widely disseminated;
- An ethics committee be set up to consider issues and conduct debate in a collegial spirit;
- Before any complaint of ethical breach is heard, the complaint be specific and accompanied by evidence;
- No financial disadvantage be brought to the complainant;
- Protection in the form of career preservation be provided;
- An 'ethical informers' (whistleblowers) support group be formed;
- The use of an independent mediator, with relevant expertise, be considered; and
- An appeal procedure be devised.

To maintain a high ethics company, every manager should:

- Behave ethically;
- Screen potential employees;
- Have a meaningful code of ethics;
- Implement ethics awareness training;
- Reinforce ethical behaviour; and
- Create a structure to deal with ethical issues.

The Use of Rewards

One of the clearly demonstrated principles of psychology is that rewards are more effective than is punishment. Rewards are reinforcers that clearly direct the person to what is considered acceptable. The difficulty with punishment is that it tells you what not to do; it does not focus on the behaviour that is desired, but only on some of the things that may not be desired. This is not to say that punishment is never effective; for example, personal boycotts are known to be a powerful technique for social control (Francis 2009).

In order for a meeting to have an agreed code, it may be helpful to adopt one, such as the one in this book, and then modify it according to the meeting's needs. In essence, a code is comprised of two parts – a code of ethics and a code of conduct. The code of ethics is a statement of the values that the meeting or its underlying organisation espouses. For example, the meeting or organisation espouses transparency, save where it protects intellectual property; compromises national security; or is personal and irrelevant. The code of conduct is a clarification of what one does or how one behaves. For example, one should never accept gifts from suppliers exceeding (say) £2, or €2, or $2 in value; likewise, one should refer all cases of potential whistleblowing to the HR department, except in cases where it might not get a fair hearing and treatment. If this should occur, it should be referred to an external and expert agency for a confidential talk, in order to receive useful advice.

Principles of Ethics

A suggested set of principles is given below (see also Francis 2009). For those with a penchant for mnemonics, as are the present writers, there is a convenient device. The principles have been arranged to read as though ethics is illuminating. The acronym is DEPHOGS (making clearer):

D = dignity
E = equitability
P = prudence
H = honesty
O = openness
G = goodwill
S = suffering (prevention and alleviation)

Dignity

Among the most important principles of ethics is that of treating each individual as an end rather than as a means to an end. However, employment does use people as a means to an end. What is asserted here is that where there is a conflict between treating people as a means to an end and treating them as ends in themselves, the latter principle should prevail.

Courtesy is also a significant component of dignity. As mentioned earlier, the way in which we commonly behave seems so appropriate that we are inclined to believe it to be morally correct. 'Good manners', whatever they may be, become prescriptive rather than just desirable.

Equitability

Equitability involves even-handedness. The essence of ethical values is that of the equitability of relationships. We admire even-handedness in meting out judgement, and highly value the principle of equitable dealing. The power held by strong commercial enterprises is moderated by the need for courtesy and dignity towards clients to be an essential part of professional work. Our legal system does the same. As the state has more power than the individual, we constrain state power by presuming innocence from wrongdoing until the contrary is proved; not trying defendants twice for the same offence (double jeopardy); not subjecting citizens to arbitrary deprivations of their liberty; requiring police to be accountable to a minister and to Parliament, and so on.

Lack of equality in power in relationships can be a source of unethical behaviour. The misuse of power unbalances a relationship. One cannot have a situation in which one side has all the rights, and the other all the duties. The equity of relationship may involve various sorts of equities, which include those of background, knowledge, and assertiveness. One might imagine an accountant and a solicitor entering a contract. Both are well-qualified professionals, and both understand the need for advice from other professionals. They consider gaining at the expense of another as a matter of acumen and not ethics. There are two principles here. One is the equality of interlocutors; the other is the equality of information. Our sense of ethics seems to require that we have a sense of equitability of both before we agree that a decision is an ethical one. Ideally, a fair judgement should be between well-informed equals; it is the absence of that equitability that arouses our concern.

Prudence

Prudence requires people to exercise a degree of judgement that makes the situation no worse, and hopefully improves the circumstances. In medicine, there is a concept called 'iatrogenesis'. This word means physician-caused illness. However, it does not necessarily mean that the physician caused the illness personally or purposely. Imagine a child with an illness requiring hospitalisation. The child is placed in an environment in which disease abounds, and might catch another disease simply by reason of being in an environment in which the risks are enhanced. It is for such situations that the ethical precept of prudence is required.

In organisational terms, one could imagine a case in which a troubleshooter visits many foreign countries. She is asked to keep watch for any information of potential benefit to her own country. After having agreed to that, she is asked to extend that watch to commercial secrets; some time later she is asked to extend it to particular commercial secrets derived from foreign, company-funded research (i.e. industrial espionage). At what point is it prudent for the troubleshooter to refuse?

Prudence – personal, corporate and national – would dictate such a decision. There must come a point when the harm outweighs the good that might be done. Prudence tells us to return to the status quo if there is any doubt. A person chairing a meeting has a casting vote, to be exercised when there is a voting tie on a motion. The convention is that the Chair will cast the vote in a cautious and prudent manner; thus an innovative motion with a tied vote will have the Chair commonly cast the vote to retain the status quo, and defeat the motion.

Honesty

The issues of honesty and openness are not always easy to distinguish. One of the few distinctions to be made is that honesty is more linked to straightforwardness and truthfulness. Its antonyms are lying, cheating, and stealing. The concept of integrity is essentially linked to that of honesty. The term is cognate with that of being whole – of being integrated. To have integrity is to have a consistency of honesty that transcends particular instances. Being honest in one situation is generalised to all situations, so that a person of integrity does not wear the hat of honesty in one forum and the hat of dishonesty in another. The attributes one would expect of a person of integrity are those of being honest (not deceitful), and of consistency of such behaviour.

Honesty is a quality that we attribute to people rather than situations. It is a quality that we (and the Oxford English Dictionary) associate with 'uprightness'. It is a generic term, which has two attributes intertwined. One is consistent behaviour; the other is behaviour conforming to key ethical principles. While consistency itself is not an ethical principle, it is what is called in philosophy a 'necessary but not sufficient condition'. Caprice and ethical behaviour are inconsistent concepts. The addition of key principles to consistency is what makes for honesty.

Openness

The essence of openness is that things should be as they purport to be, and not concealed in some casuistical manner. This principle is to be honoured in general, but not necessarily in every particular situation. An organisational representative might form the opinion that a contracting party is retreating while in a vulnerable emotional state, and that it requires support and encouragement. If the contracting party is open about this, it becomes both more and less vulnerable at once. More so in that others could take advantage of the circumstances; less so in that the disclosure invites consideration.

Openness is the quality of candour. Honesty is stating and actively being who you purport to be; openness is not concealing that which should be revealed. Even if it is not possible to reveal the information, as with commercial confidences, there is openness about the reason for nondisclosure. Insofar as we can make a distinction, these two cases of honesty and openness help distinguish the two concepts.

The caution here is that too ready a concealment may generate an attitude of paternalism ('I know best how safe genetically modified organisms are'). Paternalism, whether in the public service or the private sector, carries social dangers. It might also be noted that it is at variance with the notion of helping to develop autonomy. The advice here is to be open and honest unless there is a compelling reason not to do so.

The converse side of the openness coin is that of privacy. This is so fundamental a point that every code of ethics enshrines it. In essence, the guide is that every person and organisation has the right to personal privacy, save for special circumstances (e.g. where required by law). Here a reference to the principles of the Organisation for Economic Co-operation and Development (OECD) is appropriate.

Goodwill

Goodwill prevents many problems, helps to resolve those that do arise, and has commercial value. Most tax offices recognise that goodwill is a saleable commodity when a business is being sold. In a caring business, the existence, and the perceived existence, of goodwill are critical to successful trading. Casuistry to circumvent generous intentions, overcommitment to commercialism, and too strong a reliance on legal minima all act to circumvent best practice and generosity of spirit. In the operation of commercial enterprises, the obvious absence of goodwill makes trading both more technically difficult and less effective.

An essential aspect of goodwill is that of altruism. To be concerned for others; to be other-oriented, rather than self-oriented; and to be concerned with the greater good, rather than selfish, are all generators of goodwill. Commercial success may flow from selfless behaviour, but that is not the main reason for its being advocated here; altruism and generosity of spirit are worthy in their own right.

In modern criminological terms, would one behave better if there was a policeman ever present at one's side? Goodwill is to love one's neighbour – if not as one's self, at least to a significant degree.

Suffering

While the principles outlined so far indirectly accommodate the problem of suffering, it also useful to address the problem directly. The principles of equity and goodwill do address this issue, but only indirectly; this last principle does it directly. Suffering here is taken to mean suffering caused to any sentient being. It is not that we necessarily eschew suffering at all costs. A surgeon causes suffering, but with consent, for a higher good, and with a view to alleviating suffering in the longer term. Unwarranted suffering has no reason for existing. The consequentialist view, that pain and suffering should be prevented and alleviated, should be seen in the light of other principles, such as acting with goodwill, acting with consent, acting to reduce pain and suffering, and acting with the best interests of the organism, to whom suffering is caused. Readers wishing to know more of the background to ethics might consult Francis (2009).

Suggested Code of Conduct

Accounting procedures
> Conventional accounting procedures shall be used to maintain the financial probity of the organisation.

Account rigging
> Every account rendered in business should accurately reflect the purpose of payment for the goods or services specified. No note of indebtedness should be raised, used, or settled, unless it is open and honest.

Accounts (prompt payment of)
> See 'Bills'.

Accuracy of statements by staff
> What is stated by staff shall be consistent with what is formally written about the goods or services.

> Staff shall not make misleading statements, nor suppress relevant cautions, in order to influence behaviour.

Advertising
> See 'Public statements'.

Animal experimentation
> Activity that involves the use of animals for experimental purposes should follow the guidelines of the national body responsible for research ethics.

Anonymity of contractors
Customers, associates, and clients have a right to remain anonymous unless there is a legal duty to disclose their identities.

Anticompetitive behaviour
No contract that has the clear intent of being anticompetitive, subversive, or ill intentioned shall be entered into.

This principle is not applicable to statutory authorities, state-run business enterprises, or professions for which registration is required.

Poaching employees, customers, or clients by means other than fair and open competition is unethical.

Antisocial behaviour
No form of interchange or decisions that clearly fosters antisocial behaviour shall be used.

Beliefs or faith (duress upon)
No member or employer shall require employees or potential employees to subscribe to a particular religious faith, political viewpoint, or other ideology, in order to secure or retain a job.

Bills (prompt payment of)
Where a bill or invoice is presented, unless it is agreed otherwise, it shall be unethical not to pay that debt within 30 days. The failure to pay bills on time amounts to deprivation of capital sums due, and is unethical.

Biohazards (action issues)
Industries that have biohazardous by-products should:

- Move to least-polluting techniques of industry;
- Support research on environmental issues;
- Become energy efficient;
- Send waste for recycling;
- Use recycled wastes;
- Use least polluting cars for company fleets, and minimise car use;
- Avoid ozone-depleting substances;
- Use biodegradable materials where appropriate and possible;
- Forbid smoking on company premises and in company cars;
- Reduce toxic wastes so far as possible; and
- Exercise prudence in disposing of toxic waste.

Biohazards (policy issues)
Biohazards may be defined as those risks to the living environment that
have an impact on our capacity to survive in the longer term.

Examples of biohazards are pollutants that degrade the atmosphere, chemical
products that are illness causing, and products that are mutagenic.

This contentious area has suggested guidelines rather than prescriptions. In
order to diminish the harmful effects of biohazards, the following principles
are recommended:

- Have a written policy on biohazards.
- Set out environmental objectives in the company manual.
- Exchange information and discuss the issues with responsible groups of
  environmentally concerned people.
- Try to assess the environmental impact of products.
- Set targets for reducing adverse environmental impacts.
- Prepare a statement on environmental issues as they affect the company,
  and provide this statement with the Annual Report.
- Follow government guidelines.
- Have an external audit of the organisation's performance in biohazards.
- Set employee training programs in place to alert employees to the salient
  issues.

Blaming
The use of blame is to be avoided wherever possible.

The acceptance of personal responsibility is to be taken wherever reasonable
and possible.

Bottom line
See 'Profit'.

Bribery
Employees shall never require that jobs be bought.

The appointment to committees or jobs shall not depend on secret commissions,
promises of payment to the employer, or any other form of secret inducement.

Creating jobs for which customer tipping is the only form of payment is
unethical.

Competition
All commercial competition shall be fair, open and honest.

Computer-based information
The following are unethical:

- Introducing information into computers without the owner's permission.
- Taking information from computers without the owner's consent.
- Introducing viruses into computer systems.
- Modifying computer-based programs or information for personal gain, and without an owner's consent.

Conflict of interest
See also 'Personal gain'.

A conflict of interest occurs when a relationship, an event, or a material consideration compromises the objectivity of commercial judgement.

If there is a potential conflict of interest (personal or family relation, or friend) that might influence a commercial or business transaction or interest, it should be formally declared in writing to the appropriate person(s).

When declarations of interest are made, some written record should be retained. Examples of interests requiring declaration are: directorships, a large shareholding, promise of future employment, and employment of a close relative or friend in a position of influence in an organisation that may be given business or awarded contracts by the company.

Conflicts of interest can be avoided by:

- clarifying when the individual is speaking as a private citizen or as an employee;
- not using privileged information for personal gain;
- not having a financial interest in competitive or supplying organisations;
- not having situations that give rise to speculation as to motives;
- declaring any possible conflict of interest before the contract is agreed.

Consultants
Service entities, industry and commerce have a right to know:

- a consultant's formal qualifications;
- where those qualifications were obtained;

- details of state registration to practise as a professional;
- the amount of experience;
- specialist qualifications.

Contract breaking or evasion

Where a contract is drawn between two or more parties, and one of the parties breaks all or some of the agreement, that shall not be a justification for any of the other parties to break any of these ethical requirements.

Where a contract has been broken in such a manner, the ethical issue involved should be discussed as a matter of urgency. The use of a skilled intermediary is recommended.

Contract maintenance

Where a contract to provide goods or services has been entered, the agreement should be honoured even if in so doing the provider incurs a loss.

This principle shall not be a deterrent to the quite proper renegotiation or amendment of a contract.

Copying software

It is unethical to copy software without appropriate legal authorisation. This restriction does not apply to software in the public domain.

Copyright and patent evasion or breach

Every effort should be made to respect intellectual property in all its forms.

The use of duplicity to avoid paying royalties is unethical.

Courtesy

While endowed with the absolute right to engage in any lawful transaction, and to discuss any topic (social, religious, political, etc.), members should do so within a framework of sensitivity and tact.

Credit privacy (and information challenge)

The following guidelines are proposed:

- A credit provider should notify an individual that personal information might be disclosed to a credit reporting agency.
- Credit reporting agencies should keep information only where it is relevant to credit worthiness.

- Credit reporting agencies should not keep on file information that relates to religious or political beliefs, or sexual preference.
- It is unethical to keep credit information that is inaccurate, incomplete, or misleading.
- Credit worthiness should be used only for assessing applications for credit, assessing guarantor status, preventing financial default, or where authorised by law.
- Where a credit provider refuses an application, every assistance should be given to the applicant who wishes to challenge the information on which the decision was based. This includes giving the applicant the relevant information and its source.

Criticising

Members of committees shall avoid harshly critical statements, and odious comparisons. This does not negate the right to be critical of an idea, but the criticism should not be personal.

Cruelty to animals for luxury goods

The exploitation, pain, and slaughter of animals for non-essential purposes is to be firmly avoided.

Currency (of reference)

Where sums are quoted for any transaction, the quotation shall be in a stated currency.

If there is some compelling reason to use any other currency for any commercial transaction, the statement of the national currency used shall be unambiguous (this applies in particular to currencies that also use the term 'dollar').

Data matching

Data matching on individuals, unless legally sanctioned or permitted by the person(s), is unethical.

Deceptive information (including statistics)

It is unethical to provide deceptive information, whether through direct statement, implication, or the suppression of relevant information.

Dignity and worth

All committee transactions should be conducted in a manner consistent with human dignity and worth.

Where there is a problem, the counselling and attempted resolution shall be done constructively rather than destructively.

Statements shall not use disparagement in order to promote an idea or point of view.

Directors (special precepts)
- Directors and managers should have sufficient security of tenure and stature, such that they can disagree without fear of reprisal.
- Each director should be of such a stature and independence that he can hold the position of trust for stakeholders.
- Nonexecutive directors are not employees, and should bring special qualifications, experience, expertise, and independent perspective to the board.
- The directors' benefits should be set out explicitly.
- The audit procedures of an organisation should be set out clearly for the directors to consider.
- Directors have a duty to conserve the financial and commercial secrets of the company.
- Directors have a duty to inform the appropiate authorities of any impropriety.
- Directors have a duty to declare any conflict of interest. If necessary, directors should absent themselves from the committee or boardroom when such items are discussed.
- Directors have a responsibility to the community, consumers, employees, shareholders, carriers, and suppliers.

Disaster management plans
The speed and humanity of the response are significant determiners of an organisation's reputation. In order to keep faith with the public, an organisation at risk should consider the following:

- Institute procedures that minimise the prospect of a disaster.
- If a disaster occurs, an immediate plan should be put into operation to minimise the detrimental effects. Have someone nominated as the responsible person to handle the disaster, and appoint a spokesperson to deal with the media.
- Make a humane restitutional response to any disasters that might occur.
- Ensure that the organisation's reputation is preserved by having these appropriate policies made known to the public.

Discrimination

It is unethical to discriminate against employees on the grounds of ethnic origin, religion, race, or marital status.

It is unethical to discriminate against employees on the grounds of sex, save where there is some legal, overriding but nondenigratory, consideration (as in the acting profession, for example).

Dishonesty other than related to money

The concept of dishonesty is not confined to money matters. Its extended use covers situations in which the principles of honesty, openness, and goodwill are violated.

Dismissal

No employee should be arbitrarily dismissed.

Where an employee is to be dismissed on grounds of incompetence or lack of conscientiousness, the dismissal should only be after due warning, such that the employee can make attempts to rectify his or her behaviour.

If the dismissal is motivated by economic issues, then the need for staff reductions should be explained and acceptable solutions sought (e.g. early retirement, changing to part time, job sharing, and voluntary leaving).

Donations

Donations (particularly political ones) should be fully disclosed to all interested parties.

This shall include corporate donations.

Employer's time

The use of employer's time for personal benefit is a form of theft. Such use, unless agreed by the employer, is unethical.

The waste of an employer's time is unethical (this includes time spent for the employee's own benefit, as well as time wasted, as in cyberloafing).

Endangering species

Industry and commerce should make every effort to preserve biodiversity, and to prevent the extinction of endangered species.

Errors (admission of)
Where an error has been made, it shall be recognised and rectified.

This admission or apology should be worded in such a way as to express remorse, and offer restitution. At the same time, the action should protect the maker of the error from a legal liability, which is honestly believed to be unfounded.

Expenses (claiming unspent)
It is unethical to claim expenses that have not been incurred.

Exploitation
The exploitation of the disadvantaged (children, minority groups, the intellectually underprivileged, the disabled, those of low education, etc.) is unethical.

Falsifying figures
Under no circumstances is it ethical to falsify figures.

Financial advice
Financial advisers should be duly qualified, registered or recognised by a state or territory. If this point is not accommodated, the adviser should be a member of a reputable national body, to which the adviser owes allegiance, and whose code of professional conduct he or she is obliged to follow.

The experience of the financial adviser shall be conveyed to the client. The adviser should be covered by professional indemnity insurance (not only is the insurance important, but the process of acquiring it is a further independent check on the adviser).

An adviser must give full and free information about any benefits that the adviser might receive if the advice is followed.

Financial circumstances (personal)
When organisations recruit or promote, employers are under no ethical compulsion to consider the personal financial circumstances of the employee or potential employee.

The personal financial circumstances of employees or potential employees need not be a consideration in selecting, promoting, or increasing salary.

Foul language

Foul language is never justified. Where human frailty produces it, an apology to the target person shall be given.

This reference to human frailty shall not be taken as a common justification, bearing in mind the distinction between an irresistible impulse and an unresisted impulse.

Free quotation for goods or services

Where a free quotation for goods or services is given, and the business is not proceeded with, it shall be an ethical requirement to advise the potential supplier (the source of the quote) of the decision, and the reasons for it.

Gifts

No employee or member of his or her immediate family should accept gifts from, or give gifts to, anyone in a business relationship.

Gratuities or gifts of money, or any consideration of significant value that could be perceived as having been offered because of the business relationship, or to gain a business advantage, shall be unethical.

Gifts (advice on handling)

Gifts of a larger nature (of a value more than (say) £15 or $30) should not be given or received if they are connected to someone with whom one has a commercial relationship. The acceptance of minor tokens, calendars or diaries is quite acceptable.

All such offers should be politely but firmly declined. Gifts delivered should be returned to the sender with an appropriately worded letter, and the matter reported to a superior.

The superior may decide that the gift is to be accepted, but that it be donated elsewhere (such as a museum or a charity).

Additionally, note the following:

Any approach from a contractor, supplier or trader seeking favoured treatment in consideration of any offer of benefits or hospitality should be firmly declined and the circumstances reported to a superior, professional society, or other relevant authority.

Business entertainment should be on a reciprocal basis and on a scale consistent with what you, when host, would be authorised to arrange.

If there is the slightest doubt about accepting any offer of benefit or hospitality, it has been clearly recognised as a potentially dangerous situation and expert guidance should be sought.

The guiding principle is that one's commercial or professional objectivity should not have the possibility of being compromised.

Gossip

Gossip in the form of unsubstantiated rumours should be avoided.

This ethical restriction shall be applied to both derogatory rumours, and to information that breaches personal privacy.

Harm (do no)

Be mindful of the harmful consequences of actions in human, animal, and environmental terms. The Hippocratic notion 'Do no harm' shall be the first rule of ethics.

It is unethical to provide, or continue to provide, goods or services made for, and known to be, harmful.

Harm (goods or services intended to)

Where goods or services are clearly intended to harm, their manufacture or sale shall be unethical. Goods (such as kitchen knives, or alcoholic products) that have some other clear purpose are exempt from this precept, as are arms for defence purposes.

Harmful products (investing in)

Where a business person or organisation invests in a business that clearly provides goods or services that are in breach of this proposed code, the investing party shall draw those breaches to the attention of the offending organisation, and shall take action, as is appropriate, to minimise any harmful effects.

Healthcare providers

Company healthcare specialists and psychologists are employed as impartial advisers, and their actions governed at all times by their code of professional ethics in preference to any company or organisational code.

High-pressure sales

The use of high-pressure sales techniques is unethical. This holds true no matter what the industry is, examples being as diverse as insurance, vacuum cleaner sales, health salon services, timeshare, and mail order. The application of this principle is not restricted to new goods or services.

Industrial espionage

The use of clandestine operations to secure commercial information is unethical.

This stricture shall not apply to gathering information from the public domain. The principles of openness and honesty shall apply.

Information

General information about organisations should be freely available, except where it:

- betrays a promise;
- is embarrassing to an individual not guilty of any ethical breach;
- breaches commercial or industrial privacy; or
- might result in the loss of intellectual property.

Information (business versus personal)

Any decision on the use of personal information for valid business purposes should be weighed against an individual's right to privacy.

Information about an organisation

Confidential information about business is the property of the company. Only those people with a business need to know should have access to confidential information, and such information should not be disclosed to anyone within or outside the company without appropriate authorisation.

Information acquired during the course of work should not be disclosed outside the organisation. Information about customers and suppliers, or about any organisational individual, must not be misused.

Unless clearly understood, information gained during the course of employment that could be used to the employer's detriment must not be used either outside that employment, or in future employment with another organisation.

Information about employees

Personal information about employees must only be collected, used and retained where it is required for business or legal reasons, and should only be available to those with a clear business need to know.

Information security

Information shall be kept under secure conditions and available only to those with an agreed and legitimate right to access it.

Insider trading

Insider trading is unethical. This principle extends to any situation in which restricted information is used for personal or commercial advantage.

Intellectual property

Intellectual property is at least as valuable as physical property, and should be treated as such. Such property includes (but is not restricted to):

- Patents
- Inventions
- Industrial and commercial processes
- Creative works
- Intellectual works
- Ideas of commercial value
- Written works
- Knowledge of markets

The development and marketability of trademarks, logos and trade names is valuable intellectual (and emotional) property.

The proper use and protection of this property is an important aspect of company viability. Improperly using trademarks, or inventing misleading names or logos for a product, is unethical.

Plagiarism is unethical.

Intimidation

No form of intimidation, duress, or other improper pressures shall be used in business.

Job advertisements

All job advertisements should be genuine, and not fabricated to fulfil some other purpose.

The principle that jobs should be open to all competitors shall not be applied to family businesses, but in such cases the situation should be made clear.

Nepotism is not unethical in family companies, but is so in other organisations.

The guiding principle is that employment described in job advertisements should be what it purports to be.

Job selection criteria
Where an organisation is not a family one, the use of other than the best objective selection criteria for job performance is unethical.

Labelling
Labelling of products should be accurate and sufficiently comprehensive as to be a useful guide to consumers.

Language of commerce
The forced use of a language other than the language of the nation is socially divisive and fraught with the possibility of misunderstanding. Social cohesion is fostered by, *inter alia*, a common means of communication.

The primary language of commerce should be that of the country in question, and it is unethical to use any argument that subverts this principle.

This principle does not require that no other language be used in addition, but asserts that English is the reference language.

This principle shall not prevent those of alien tongue from engaging in commerce using their own common language.

The public, employees, suppliers and consumers have a right to information in plain language. Such information shall be free of undue technicalities and obfuscations, and shall be, as far as possible, in plain prose.

Law (dealing with)
It is not the function of a code of business conduct to change the law. Rather, it is to fill gaps in the law, and to express the business values of the national society in particular, and of generous-spirited humanity in general.

If a matter is illegal, then the law prevails over ethical considerations.

It is unethical to act or advise in any way that produces a contravention of state or federal law.

If the law is seen to be inadequate, mistaken, outdated or ambiguous, the proper legally sanctioned procedures should be followed in order to have the law amended. It is not the primary function of this code to press for changes to the law, although ethical arguments may well be the basis for legitimate pressure to amend the law.

It is unethical to use threats of litigation, involving either costly cases or public embarrassment, as a means of gaining commercial advantage.

The use of legal tactics to delay the resolution of ethical dilemmas is unethical.

Misrepresentation

No statement, explicit or implicit, shall misrepresent the nature of goods or services involved in any sort of commerce.

Misrepresentation includes statements asserted and implied, and the suppression of critical information.

Monopoly

Except where sanctioned by law, it is unethical to be a monopoly supplier of either goods or services.

Personal gain

No employees should be involved in activity for personal gain that, for any reason, is in conflict with the business interest of organisations for which they work.

No work shall be solicited or performed by employees or consultants that could be in competition with the organisations with which they are engaged.

Unless authorised by a director or a principal, no outside work should be performed, nor businesses or clients solicited, in company time or on company premises.

Company-owned equipment, materials, resources or inside information shall not be used for outside work without appropriate authorisation.

Personal information (use of)

Personal information should not be collected without good ethical reason.

Personal information collected for one purpose should not be used for another (except for research under certain specified conditions, such as with the owner's consent, or as required by law).

Trading data and trafficking in personal information, except as permitted by law, is unethical.

Selling names and addresses without the permission of the persons concerned is unethical.

Personal violence

Personal violence in the pursuit of business ends is unethical.

Nonhuman animals shall be treated in such a manner as to minimise suffering.

The use of animals for tests on nonessentials (e.g. cosmetics) is unethical.

Personnel selection information

No confidential information gained in personnel work or selection information may be disclosed to others without the consent of the person who is the subject of that information.

No psychological test data used for one purpose or job selection shall be used for another job application, or other purpose.

Pollution

Industry and commerce should attempt to devise and use the least-polluting strategies in the exercise of their businesses.

Praise

When giving feedback of any kind, the use of positive statements, praise, and encouragement are to be preferred to negative and punitive approaches.

Prevention

In order to prevent breaches of ethics, the following measures are suggested:

- Senior management to set a good example.
- Training programs in ethical behaviour in business be provided.
- Seminars on business ethics be commissioned.

- One of the staff selection criteria be ethical commitment.
- Rewards for ethical commitment be provided.
- An ethical audit be a part of annual reporting (institutionalised reporting).

Pricing in advance of increased costs

Where a price rise has been announced, the goods or stock bought at the lesser price shall be the basis of the selling price. Only when the more expensive goods or stock are traded shall the price increase apply.

Privacy (customer)

Customers' privacy and confidences shall be maintained except where there is an overriding legal obligation to reveal.

Privacy (employee)

The recognition of employees' personal privacy is an ethical imperative.

Privacy (general principles)

Every person has the right to personal privacy, save where divulgence is required by law. The Organisation for Economic Co-operation and Development has set out eight principles on privacy:

Collection limitation: There should be limits on the collection of personal data. It should be done lawfully, fairly and, where appropriate, with the person's consent.

Data quality: Data collected should be relevant to the purpose and kept up to date.

Specified purpose: People should be told why the data is being collected, and it should not be used for purposes incompatible with the stated purpose.

Use limitation: Personal data should not generally be used or disclosed in ways the individual does not know about, except with the authority of law.

Security safeguards: Personal data should be given reasonable security against unauthorised access, destruction, use or changes.

Openness: People should be able to find out easily what is held on them, what it is used for, and who controls it.

Individual participation: People should be able to see data held on them (or be given reasons for any refusal) and be able to challenge what is in it.

Accountability: Data controllers should be accountable for their compliance with the principles.

Private inquiry agents

Investigations by private inquiry agents shall only be used defensively (not offensively).

Where such defensive information is collected, it shall be used only for that purpose, and shall be adequately protected against use for any other purpose.

Clandestine surveillance, wire tapping, bugging, and any other means of eavesdropping, except as sanctioned by law, is unethical.

Profit

Profit-making organisations are mindful of their obligations to maximise their profits. This motive, to maximise profit, should not be at the expense of keeping to the principles of ethical behaviour.

Property (respect for organisation's)

An organisation's property is more than its physical plant and equipment, or product. It includes technologies and concepts, ideas and recipes, and business and product plans, as well as general information about the business.

Misappropriation of the company's property in any form is unethical.

Provisional allowances in contracts

Where provisional allowances are made in contracts, the upper limits shall be defined.

Public statements

Public statements about an organisation should only be made by those authorised to do so.

Advertisements emanating from an organisation shall be authorised only by those empowered to do so. Someone known to be connected with an organisation, but speaking as a private individual, should make this distinction clear.

When making a public statement in which conflict of interest may be an issue, such conflict of interest should be made clear.

Prospectuses and information sheets must contain factually accurate statements.

Prospectuses and information sheets must not suppress important, relevant information.

Where possibly disadvantageous information needs to be asserted, it should have prominence equal to that of the advantageous material (i.e. no small print).

Quality of goods and services

Manufacturers shall strive to provide excellence in goods. This principle shall extend to after-sales service.

Where the goods or services provided are in need of remedy, such remedy shall be conducted with efficiency, despatch and courtesy.

Racist regimes

Although it may be necessary to deal with foreign regimes that are racist and sexist, those who do so should take effort to minimise any harm, and should try to modify those racist and sexist views.

Redundancies and relocation

Relocation of employees within an organisation, including geographical relocation, shall be discussed with the employees concerned. Any available options should be outlined.

Redundancies of employees within an organisation should be discussed with the employees concerned. Such discussions should outline the reasons for the proposal, and what options are available.

Reliable products

Reliability of products shall be one of the main concerns of manufacturers.

Sabotage

Sabotage may be defined as the 'intentional malicious damage or harm to work, commercial or industrial connections, or to equipment by employees in dispute with management.' Sabotage is unethical.

Safety standards

Where the ethical precepts of very high-level safety standards conflict with the standards of other nations or cultures with lower standards, the safer standard shall prevail.

In addition to following legislation on occupational health and safety, employers should be mindful of the intent of such legislation. If an action or inaction is foreseen to result in harm, no matter what the legislation holds, not to undertake preventive action is unethical.

Safe practices

It is difficult to be exact about 'harm'. Clearly a product that is unsafe, or does not do what it purports to do, is unethical. The difficulty arises with products that do exactly what they purport to do, but the purpose is harmful (e.g. bullets or napalm).

The guiding principle here is that, if the public expects a particular product to perform in a certain way, that performance should not be attended by harm not clearly notified.

Secret commissions

It is unethical to take secret commissions or to solicit or receive compromising gifts. This includes such diverse practices as: secret commissions for real estate agents; tour operators taking tourists to places where the operator's commission is given (and not disclosed to the tourists); and secret commissions made in the expectation of business.

Sexual favours

Except where that is the explicit purpose of a business (as in brothels), the use of sex for business purposes is unethical.

Shareholders (right to information)

Shareholders have the right to know executive remuneration and severance packages, and information about the directors' achievements, salary, and perquisites.

Smoking and employment

Being a smoker should not be a bar to employment, but if there are good reasons for preferring a nonsmoker, it is not unethical to make such a discrimination.

Taking credit
It is unethical to take improper credit for the work or achievements of others.

Taxes and imposts (removal of)
Where a state government or a federal government reduces or removes a tax or impost on goods or services, the consequent savings shall be immediately passed on in full to the consumer.

Tipping
An obligation to tip is unethical.

This precept shall not invalidate the notion of a reward for exceptional service in the hospitality industry, but tipping is to be generally discouraged.

The imposition of a service charge by managerial fiat is unethical.

Vulnerable customers and traders
It is unethical to commercially target the vulnerable.

Withdrawal of harmful goods or services
Where it comes to the attention of providers of goods or services that their products are harmful, the goods or services should be withdrawn from sale and/or recalled.

Measurement of Outcomes

In order to monitor progress, one might design a series of ethical goals and strategies to execute, the achievements of which can act as the basis for a measurement scheme. Such goals and strategies could include:

• Translation into behaviour (actually do ethical things in ethically ambiguous situations);
• Provision of precise ethical-learning goals to staff (master the company code by a certain date);
• Communication on how the achievement of ethical goals contributes to self-worth and company profile;
• Creation of new ways of judging ethical performance, and provision of appropriate nontangible rewards (such as honourable mention).

Concrete measurement of the translation of the code into behaviour may be achieved by asking some specific questions, such as the following:

- How many insider trade deals were done?
- How many technical breaches occurred?
- How many 'sweeteners' were given?
- How many customers were misled?
- How many union principles were breached?
- How many occupational health and safety measures were breached?

Part Four

SAMPLES OF RELEVANT PAPERS

Introduction

This section consists of three types of documents: constitutions, agendas, and minutes. They are presented in good faith as examples of how such documents commonly look. It should be understood that they are paradigmatic instances, designed to be modified to fit a particular institutional need.

CONSTITUTIONS

Constitution 1: The International Society of Social Professionals

30th June 2010

The International Society of Social Professionals (hereinafter referred to as *The Society*) exists to provide a supportive organisational structure to further the aims of fumdumbulating, and its commercial applications. As such, *The Society* has recognition by the appropriate corporate authorities, a funding base and income, and a budget. The invention of The Society provides a forum for discussions of fumdumbulation.

In addition to paid staff, there are volunteers who provide their services freely, and whose actions for *The Society* are covered by *The Society* insurance policy.

The Society has an agreed Code of Ethics and Code of Conduct to which all connected with *The Society* must subscribe (attached; see also 4.1.) Where formal meetings take place, the rules governing the conduct of such meetings shall be approved by the Board at the Annual General Meeting (AGM) (attached). *The Society* has a policy governing whistleblowing, and an extended expression of the policy (attached).

FIRST PART – Responsibilities

On behalf of all stakeholders of *The Society*, and especially the members, the Board is responsible for the stewardship and future wellbeing of the *The Society*. The Board should exercise leadership, enterprise, integrity and judgement in directing *The Society*, so as to provide assurance of its continuing and lasting function. Members should endeavour to achieve the highest possible standards of corporate governance. The meeting should always act in the best interests of *The Society*, and in a manner based on transparency, accountability and responsibility.

In discharging their responsibilities, the Board and individual members have a duty to act in the best interests of *The Society* as a whole, irrespective of personal, professional, commercial or other interests, loyalties or affiliations. When serving as members, the first duty and loyalty must be to *The Society*.

Governance defines the role of the Board. Governance might be described as:

> The exercise of corporate leadership, through the establishment and monitoring of necessary controls and strategic direction setting, so that *The Society* is equipped to respond to changing circumstances and situations in the external and internal environments, in order to meet the expectations and demands of members and other key stakeholders.

The Board establishes *The Society*'s purpose, values, goals and objectives; employs the Chief Executive Officer; identifies and monitors the management of corporate risks; and monitors and assesses Chief Executive Officer and organisation performance.

In brief, governance involves the Board in the process of ensuring that *The Society* is well managed, without the Board itself becoming involved in the operations – except as required by its legislation, or as a consequence of exceptional circumstances.

Governance is Different from Management

Whereas the Board sets governance-level policies and establishes the strategic direction – including the development of *The Society* purpose, values, goals and objectives – the Chief Executive Officer designs and manages the processes that ensure that these policies and directives are honoured or met. The Chief Executive Officer is thus the agent of the Board. The Board is responsible for determining the 'What' and the 'Why', and the Chief Executive Officer is responsible for determining the 'How'. Another way to consider the difference between the two roles is to think of the Board's role as being to determine organisational 'Ends', or outcomes, and the Chief Executive Officer's role to design the 'Means', or methods to achieve those ends.

Two Levels of Organisational Policy

Governance-level policy

Policies at this level are developed and adopted by the Board, and relate to high-level, organisation-wide matters. These include policies in respect of the Board's operating processes and duties, and its delegation to the Chief Executive Officer in areas such as finances, human resources management, public affairs and asset management. These policies are a reflection of the Board's desire to meet its Duty of Care under law and its moral responsibility to provide good governance on behalf of all interested parties.

Management-level policy

These are developed by the Chief Executive Officer, and relate to the operational management of *The Society*. The Board is not required to approve policies at this level. Management-level policies flow logically from governance policies.

SECOND PART – Responsibilities of the Board

Enacting the governance responsibilities

The Board is responsible for protecting the rights and interests of the members, and is accountable to them for the overall management of *The Society*.

In discharging its obligations and duties, the Board should assume responsibility in at least the following areas:

Meeting legal requirements

The Board's first duty is to *The Society*. In meeting this duty, the Board must ensure that *The Society* meets all legal requirements under the relevant acts, and is protected from harmful situations and circumstances, as in acting in the interests of current and future stakeholders. The Board also has a responsibility to its various stakeholders to ensure that the available resources are used in order to deliver the 'right outcomes' to the 'right people' in the 'right way'.

In particular the Board has the following obligations:

- To act in good faith in the interests of all stakeholders of *The Society*
- To exercise its powers towards a proper purpose
- To avoid conflicts of interests
- To act honestly
- To act with reasonable care and diligence
- Not to allow members to make improper use of either their position on the Board or of information gained while in that role
- To hold members, both individually and collectively, potentially liable if they act illegally or negligently

Board membership

The Board will:

1. Ensure that potential candidates are fully conversant with the role, responsibilities, work programme and performance of the Board and its members;
2. Provide a thorough orientation process for new Board members;
3. Ensure that all potential Board members sign a declaration acknowledging their responsibilities as a Board member of *The Society*, in a form agreed upon by the Board.

Governance philosophy and approach

The Board will govern *The Society* with emphasis on:

1. A future focus rather than a preoccupation with the present or past;
2. Strategic issues rather than administrative detail;
3. Proactivity rather than reactivity;
4. Encouraging a diversity of opinions and views;
5. The development and expression of a collective responsibility for all aspects of the Board's performance;
6. Continuing improvement of *The Society*, Board and individual Board member effectiveness, and the interests of *The Society* as a whole;
7. Ensuring Board decisions treat all members fairly;
8. Monitoring the effectiveness of the governance policies under which the Board operates, and making changes as required.

Strategic leadership: Insight and foresight

The Board will:

1. Formulate, authorise and monitor *The Society*'s vision, mission and strategic objectives.
2. Understand the strategic context, and monitor *The Society*'s role within it.
3. Recommend any significant shifts in the broad strategic direction of *The Society* to the members.
4. Monitor performance against the strategic direction, including assessing operating results in order to evaluate whether the business is being properly managed.
5. Provide input that assists in identifying and understanding emerging trends and issues likely to affect the wellbeing of *The Society* and its members.
6. Review *The Society*'s situation and agree upon the broad framework within which the strategic and business plans will be prepared each year.

Operating performance: Oversight

The Board will:

1. Ensure the development and review of annual business plans.
2. Review the progress of *The Society*'s attainment of its five-year strategic plan, with a major review to be conducted every three years.
3. Review and approve *The Society*'s financial objectives, plans and actions, including significant capital allocations and expenditures.
4. Ensure that there are adequate internal controls and ethical standards of behaviour.

Risk management

Risk management might be defined as:

> A logical and systematic method of identifying, analysing, assessing, treating, and communicating risks associated with any activity, function or process in a way that will enable an organisation to minimise losses and maximise opportunities.

The Board will identify and evaluate the principal risks faced by *The Society* and ensure that appropriate systems are in place to avoid or mitigate these risks, including the protection of intellectual capital.

Direction of executive performance

The Board will:

1. Select, monitor and, if necessary, replace the Chief Executive Officer;
2. Maintain an up-to-date framework for defining the Board's expectations of the Chief Executive Officer's performance, including the setting of a clear, annual performance agreement;
3. Provide regular, honest and rigorous performance feedback to the Chief Executive Officer on the achievement of such expectations;
4. Ensure there are positive conditions for the motivation of the Chief Executive Officer, and ensure that there is adequate training to support her/him in the role;
5. Establish a list of levels and types of expenditure that the Chief Executive Officer must bring to the Board.

Compliance and integrity

The Board will:

1. Ensure ethical behaviour, and compliance with state and federal laws and regulations; audit and accounting principles; and *The Society*'s stated values and governance documents;
2. Ensure the integrity of *The Society*'s internal control and management information systems, so that its decision-making capability and the accuracy of its reporting are maintained at a high level at all times.

Board focus

The Board will:

1. Ensure that the Board makes the best possible use of its meetings by dealing only with matters that have governance-level significance; by focusing primarily on the future; and, within a defined policy framework, by delegating as much as possible to the Chief Executive Officer;
2. Ensure that reports and proposals that come to the Board reflect the Board's governance role. Among other things they must be timely, clearly identify the proposed resolution, and usually be less than an A4 page in length.

Board meetings

As a general rule, the Board will meet monthly, but at least no less than bimonthly.

The Chair in conjunction with the Chief Executive Officer will establish the agenda for each Board meeting, although each Board member is free to suggest the inclusion of item(s) on the agenda. To the extent possible (given that some matters worthy of the Board's attention may be unforeseen) agendas will be based on a schedule of subjects agreed upon at the beginning of each year, and documented in the form of an annual work agenda.

Monitoring and enhancing Board effectiveness

The Board will annually assess its own effectiveness in fulfilling this charter and other Board responsibilities, including the effectiveness of individual Board members.

Assurance of accountability

The Board willensure that it is kept informed of the relevant views and interests of:

1. The general public outside the fundumbulation world;
2. Those within key fundumbulation worlds;
3. The members, specifically regarding their concerns, needs and aspirations;
4. The present members of *The Society*, specifically regarding their legitimate collective interests, for which the Board will serve and account fully.

The Board will also report to an annual meeting of the members on the performance of all *The Society*'s entities, and account for the Board's stewardship of that performance.

Interaction with the media

In all contact with the media, the Chief Executive Officer or her/his delegate shall be the sole spokesperson on all operating matters relating to *The Society*. The Chair of the Board will be the alternative spokesperson as mutually agreed upon with the Chief Executive Officer.

Other

The Board will perform other functions as prescribed by law or as assigned to the Board under *The Society*'s governing documents.

THIRD PART – Expectations of Board Members

To execute these governance responsibilities, Board members must, as far as possible, ensure that they possess certain characteristics, abilities and understandings. To support these responsibilities, appropriate training and support will be provided.

Board member responsibilities

- Board members must fulfil their fiduciary duty to act in *The Society*'s best interest at all times, regardless of personal position, circumstances, or affiliation. They must be familiar with *The Society*'s constitutional arrangements and be aware of, and fulfil, the statutory and fiduciary responsibilities of a Board member.
- Board members must act in accordance with the Code of Ethics and Code of Conduct, and with conflict of interest policies.
- Board members are expected to be punctual and to attend Board meetings regularly for their full extent – and be willing to contribute outside of meetings if required. They should come to Board meetings fully prepared.
- For a member to remain on a committee or the Board, he/she should be required to attain a minimum attendance in person (say, 75 per cent of meetings). Where such attendance requirements are not met, then the member is removed from membership and replaced. When so removed from membership, the person who failed to attend is disbarred from being eligible for membership again until the next election or appointment.

Strategic orientation

Board members should be future oriented, demonstrating vision and foresight. They are expected to think conceptually, taking a 'helicopter' or 'big-picture' perspective. They should be able to synthesise and simplify complex information and ideas. Their focus should be on strategic goals and policy implications rather than operational detail. They need to understand and focus on issues that are central to the success of *The Society*.

Integrity and accountability

Board members must demonstrate high ethical standards and integrity in their personal and professional dealings, and be willing to act on – and remain collectively accountable for – all Board decisions, even if unpopular or if individual members disagree with them. Board members must be committed to speaking with one voice on all policy and directional matters.

Informed and independent judgement

Each member of the Board must have the ability to provide wise, thoughtful counsel on a broad range of issues. He or she must have (or be able to develop) a sufficient depth of knowledge about *The Society*'s business. This is in order to understand and question the assumptions upon which strategic and business plans and important proposals are based, and to be able to form an independent judgement as to the probability that such plans can be achieved, or proposals successfully implemented. Each Board member must be willing to risk losing rapport with fellow Board members in taking a reasoned, independent position.

Financial literacy

Because the Board must monitor financial performance, Board members must be financially literate. They should be able to read financial statements and understand the use of financial ratios and other indices used for evaluating *The Society*'s performance.

Participation

Each Board member is expected to enhance the Board's deliberations by actively offering questions and comments that add value to the discussion. Each should strive to be at ease with fellow Board members, participating in a constructive manner that acknowledges and respects the contributions of others at the table, including the executive team. Board members must be able to accept challenges from others without becoming defensive. In order to foster teamwork and engender trust, Board members should be willing to reconsider or change their positions after hearing statements of others' reasoned viewpoints.

Whistleblowing

In order to honour its duty to protect *The Society* against harmful situations and circumstances, the Board will provide a safe channel for volunteers and staff members to bring to its attention information about acts, omissions or decisions of a serious nature that could threaten *The Society*'s integrity. Accordingly, any volunteer or staff member will have access to the Board when there is evidence or reasonable (i.e. soundly based) suspicion that the Chief Executive Officer has:

1. Breached a Board policy;
2. Allowed other staff or volunteers to breach Board policies; or
3. Acted or allowed staff or volunteers to act in a manner likely to cause serious harm to *The Society*.

This is, in effect, a 'whistleblower' provision. The channel to the Board in such a circumstance will be via the Board Chair. Any assertion will be formally noted by the Board. All individuals involved in such an action will have the protection of natural justice. Provided that, in the judgement of the Board, the claim is not vexatious or frivolous, the staff member or volunteer bringing a whistleblowing assertion against the Chief Executive Officer shall be protected against discrimination for having taken such an action.

FOURTH PART – Governance Policies

The Board will be committed to the adoption of ethical conduct in all areas of its responsibilities and authority.

Code of Ethics and proper practice

The Board shall:

1. Act honestly and in good faith at all times, and in the best interests of *The Society* members as a whole;
2. Declare all interests that could result in a conflict between personal and organisational priorities;
3. Exercise diligence and care in fulfilling the functions of office;
4. Attend Board meetings and devote sufficient time to prepare for Board meetings, in order to provide full and appropriate participation in the Board's decision making;
5. Put the needs of *The Society* before members' own needs;
6. Ensure scrupulous avoidance of deception, unethical practice or any other behaviour that is, or might be construed as, less than honourable in the pursuit of *The Society*'s business;
7. Not disclose to any other person confidential information other than as agreed by the Board or as required under law;
8. Act in accordance with its fiduciary duties, comply with the spirit as well as the letter of the law, and recognise both the legal and moral duties of the role;
9. Abide by Board decisions once reached, notwithstanding a Board member's right to pursue a review or reversal of a Board decision;
10. Not comment, issue, authorise, offer or endorse any public criticism or statement having or designed to have an effect prejudicial to the best interests of *The Society*.

The Board shall:

1. Ensure that there is an appropriate separation of duties and responsibilities between itself and its Chief Executive Officer;
2. Make every reasonable effort to ensure that *The Society* does not raise community, supplier or stakeholder expectations beyond that which can be fulfilled;
3. Meet its responsibility to ensure that all staff and volunteers employed by *The Society* are treated with due respect and provided with a working environment and working conditions that meet all reasonable standards of employment as defined in relevant workplace legislation;
4. Regularly review its own performance as the basis for its own development and quality assurance;
5. Carry out its meetings in such a manner as to ensure fair and full participation of all Board members;
6. Ensure that *The Society*'s assets are protected via a suitable risk-management strategy.

Conflicts of interests

- The Board places great importance on making clear any existing or potential conflicts of interest for Board members.
- Any business or personal matter that could lead to a conflict of interest of a material nature involving a Board member and his/her role and relationship with *The Society* must be declared and registered in a register of interest.
- All such entries in the register shall be presented to the Board and minuted at the first Board meeting following entry in the records.
- All conflicts of interest must be declared by the Board member concerned at the earliest time after the conflict is identified.
- The Board shall determine whether or not the conflict is of a material nature, and shall advise the individual accordingly.
- Where a conflict of interest is identified and/or registered and the Board declares that it is of material benefit to the individual or of material significance to *The Society*, the Board member concerned shall not vote on any resolution relating to that conflict or issue.
- The Board member shall only remain in the room during any related discussion with Board approval.
- The Board will determine which records and other documentation relating to the matter will be available to the Board member concerned. All such occurrences will be minuted.

- Individual Board members aware of a real or potential conflict of interest of another Board member have a responsibility to bring it to the notice of the Board.

Conflicts of interest may occur:

1. When a Board member, or his/her immediate family or business interests, stands to gain financially from any business dealings, programmes or services provided to *The Society*;
2. When a Board member offers a professional service to *The Society*;
3. When a Board member stands to gain personally or professionally from any insider knowledge and uses that knowledge for personal or professional advantage.

Board committees and working parties

- The Board will establish committees and working parties only to support it in its own work, and never to conflict with the Chief Executive Officer's delegated responsibilities.
- Committees and working parties shall have terms of reference and/or role definitions– clearly defining their role, life span, procedures and functions, and the boundaries of their authority – which shall be reviewed annually.
- Unless explicitly empowered by the Board, committees or working parties cannot make binding Board decisions or speak for the Board. For the most part, the function of committees and working parties is to make recommendations to the Board.
- A decision of a committee or working party exercising delegated authority is a decision of the Board, and should be treated by the Chief Executive Officer accordingly.
- Committees and working parties may co-opt outside members from time to time in order to bring additional skills, experience or networks.
- Committees and working parties can neither exercise authority over staff or volunteers, nor delegate tasks to any staff or volunteers, unless the Chief Executive Officer has specifically agreed to such delegations.
- Committees and working parties will not mirror operational divisions, departments, staff or volunteer functions.

FIFTH PART – Audit and Risk Committee: Terms of Reference

Committee objective

The objective of the Audit and Risk Committee is to assist the Board in discharging its responsibilities, with respect to overseeing all aspects of financial and nonfinancial reporting, control and audit functions, and organisational risk.

Membership

- The Audit and Risk Committee shall be appointed by the Board from amongst Board members, and shall consist of at least three members.
- The convenor of the Audit and Risk Committee shall be appointed by the Board.
- The Committee shall be structured to include members with (1) financial skills, including the ability to read and analyse financial statements; (2) a good understanding of business and financial risks, and of related controls and control processes; (3) a sound knowledge of the industry; and (4) a commitment to core service-delivery principles and practices.
- A quorum shall be three members, one of whom shall be the convenor or his/her delegate.

Operating principles

- The Committee may have in attendance members of management and other such persons that it deems necessary to provide appropriate information and explanations.
- The Board shall be entitled to attend all meetings of the Audit and Risk Committee.
- The Committee shall have the right to go 'in committee' as required.
- The convenor shall call a meeting of the Audit and Risk Committee if so requested by any Committee member, the Board, the internal management or the external auditors.
- The convenor shall have drawn up an agenda to be circulated at least one week prior to each meeting. The agenda shall be distributed to the members of the Committee, the external auditors and other invitees.
- The accountants, senior managers and external auditors shall be given adequate notice of all meetings and shall have the right to attend and speak.
- Meetings shall be held at least four times each year, or as and when necessary. Meetings are to be held (1) at the planning stage of the external audit; (2) prior to the Board meeting for approving the annual report and financial statements; and (3) at scheduled times during the year in accordance with the Committee's planned programme.
- The Committee will review an annual audit plan and recommend its approval or rejection by the Board.
- The Committee is authorised to obtain external resources as required to assist with its work. Any expenditure will be limited by the existing delegation of authority, unless endorsed by the Board.
- The Committee will give notice to management of its programme and its requirements for access to key financial and other personnel records, and any others considered relevant.

- The Committee shall report to the Board after each Committee meeting, or as specified or requested by the Board. Committee meetings shall be minuted, of which a copy shall be tabled at the following Board meeting. Additionally, the Committee shall submit an annual report to the Board summarising the Committee's activities during the year, and the related significant results and findings.
- The Committee shall annually conduct an assessment of its effectiveness and of the contributions of individual Committee members. Changes in personnel, roles or responsibilities shall be determined by the Board.

Responsibilities

The duties of the Audit and Risk Committee are as follows:

1. Identify the broad risk parameters within which *The Society* operates, and bring to the Board's notice all such risks as the Committee feels should be addressed by the Board;
2. Oversee and monitor the effectiveness of the Chief Executive Officer's risk-management programme and periodically report to the Board on the effectiveness of this;
3. Work in liaison with internal and external auditors;
4. Review the annual audit plan with the auditors, and oversee the rotation of the principal audit partner;
5. Review audit findings and annual financial statements;
6. Review the integrity of the Chief Executive Officer's financial and nonfinancial reporting to the Board;
7. Oversee compliance with statutory responsibilities relating to financial and nonfinancial disclosure;
8. Review internal financial systems and accountabilities;
9. Ensure that recommendations highlighted in the internal audit reports (if any) are actioned by management;
10. Supervise special investigations in areas of financial and nonfinancial performance when requested by the Board.

In addition, the Audit and Risk Committee shall examine any other matters referred to it by the Board.

Authority

The Committee is authorised by the Board to investigate any activity covered by its functions and responsibilities. It is authorised to seek any information it requires from the Chief Executive Officer, who shall cooperate with any request made by the Committee.

The Committee shall have the authority of the Board to obtain legal or other independent professional advice, and to secure the attendance at meetings of third parties with relevant experience and expertise if it considers this necessary. Any expenditure will be limited by the existing delegation of authority, unless endorsed by the Board.

The Audit and Risk Committee shall have no executive powers with regards to its findings and recommendations, other than those bestowed by the Board.

SIXTH PART – Board Processes

Agenda planning

To meet the standards of good governance, the Board will follow a one-year agenda that (1) regularly reviews results, policies and relevant strategic issues; (2) provides assurance that all relevant compliance requirements are addressed; and (3) improves Board performance through education and continuous focus on its governance effectiveness.

The Board will develop an annual agenda setting out a framework for its year's work. Examples of recurring and once-off agenda items include:

Review of SMART (Specific, Measurable, Achievable, Realistic, Timely) goals.

Scheduled review of Board-stated results, as indicated in the Board's strategic planning statements, e.g. via Chief Executive Officer reports and presentations.

Scheduled time for strategic thinking

Governance education as appropriate, e.g. sessions that facilitate a better understanding of the governance of *The Society* and the directors' duties and liabilities.

Board effectiveness review

Assessment of Board effectiveness can include:

1. Consultations with key stakeholders as appropriate
2. Scheduled assessment of organisational risk

3. Scheduled reporting by the Audit Committee or other Board committees
4. Other policy compliance monitoring, both in respect of Chief Executive Officer delegation and other Board policies, e.g. regular financial and nonfinancial reporting

Meeting with the external auditor

The external auditor reports to the Board Audit Committee. Items for discussion include:

- Chief Executive Officer performance-appraisal review meetings (setting up and reporting) and remuneration review.
- Specific Board discussion relating to projects currently underway, e.g. buildings, change programmes, etc.
- Preparation for, or review of, AGM matters.
- All other matters that the Board can plan for.

New Board member induction

The Board will provide all new Board members a thorough induction into the affairs of both the Board and *The Society* at large.

All prospective Board members will be provided with all relevant information.

Prior to attendance at their first Board meeting, new Board members will:

1. Receive a copy of the Board's resource handbook, including governance policies, the Articles/Constitution and other relevant legal governance documentation, as well as current and recent meeting papers, an organisational chart, contact details for other Board members and key staff and volunteers, a glossary of key terms, definitions and acronyms, the current year's meeting schedule and the annual agenda;
2. Meet with the Chair for a governance familiarisation. This meeting may be held as a group session or on an individual basis;
3. Meet with the Chief Executive Officer for an operational familiarisation. This meeting may be held as a group session or on an individual basis.

Board development

The Board's value-adding role requires that all Board members have access to professional development relevant to their duties as Board members. The Board will make every reasonable effort to facilitate training for all Board members and for the Board as a whole, in order to maximise its value-adding contribution to *The Society*.

The Board will annually carry out a review of its performance. The Board may engage outside assistance to assist in fulfilling its monitoring responsibilities. This includes, but is not limited to, financial audit.

All costs associated with governance effectiveness will be sufficient to meet the development of the highest standard of governance, including meeting costs associated with effective communication with owners and other key stakeholders; surveys and associated analysis; focus groups; the costs associated with external audit, and other independent third party reviews; and consulting input.

Chair role

- The Chair provides leadership to the Board, ensuring that the Board's processes and actions are consistent with its policies.
- As appropriate, the Chair represents the Board and *The Society* to outside parties.
- The Chair is empowered to chair Board meetings.
- The meetings' discussion content will be confined to governance matters, as defined in the Board's policies.
- All Board members will be treated even-handedly and fairly.
- All Board members will be encouraged and enabled to make a contribution to the Board's deliberations.
- There may be times when the Chair is called upon to interpret a Board policy, or policies to outside parties, or policies when in the absence of the Board. All such interpretations shall reflect both the stated intent and spirit of the policy/ies.
- The Chair has no authority to unilaterally change any aspect of Board policy.
- The Chair will establish a regular communication arrangement with the Chief Executive Officer, during which there is an exchange of information. This might also provide an opportunity for the Chief Executive Officer to use such sessions as a sounding board for proposed actions, or to check interpretations of Board policy.

However:

- The Chair will recognise that such sessions are not used to 'personally' supervise or direct the Chief Executive Officer, except when he/she has breached Board policy.

- The Chair will not inhibit the free flow of information to the Board necessary for sound governance. Therefore the Chair will never come between the Board and its formal links with the Chief Executive Officer.
- The Chair may delegate aspects of the authority accompanying the position, but remains accountable for the overall role.

Indemnities and insurance

- *The Society* will provide Board members with indemnity cover while acting in their capacities as Board members, to the fullest extent permitted by the relevant legislation.
- *The Society* will provide Board members with, and pay premiums for, indemnity insurance to an amount as determined by the Board or a specially convened committee of the Board.

Reimbursement of Board members' expenses

The Society will reimburse all reasonable expenses incurred by Board members in the carrying out of their role. The Chief Executive Officer will provide details of all reimbursement to Board members at the next Board meeting.

SEVENTH PART – Board–Chief Executive Officer Interrelationship Policies

Responsibilities of the Chief Executive Officer

The Chief Executive Officer shall:

- Act honestly, diligently, and competently at all times in the fulfilment of his/her duties and responsibilities. In so doing the Chief Executive Officer shall use his/ her best endeavours to promote and protect the interests of *The Society*. For the avoidance of doubt, it is recorded that the duties and responsibilities of the Chief Executive Officer are required to be performed at the premises of *The Society* and elsewhere as required.
- Be responsible for discharging all duties and responsibilities hereunder, at all times during the normal hours of *The Society* and at such other times as may reasonably be required by the Board, having regard to the duties and responsibilities of the position.
- Exercise all the rights, duties and powers that are conferred upon the Chief Executive Officer from time to time by any enactment, or by delegation from the Board.

- Promote compliance with all statutory obligations imposed upon *The Society*, the Board, or upon employees.
- Do all such incidental things consistent with the position of Chief Executive Officer, as are reasonably necessary for the proper performance of the duties and responsibilities of the role.
- Carry out and comply with all reasonable and lawful directions given by the Board or by any person authorised by the Board to give such directions.
- Undertake such duties and exercise such powers, authority and discretion in relation to the business of *The Society* as may from time to time be delegated to the Chief Executive Officer.
- Undertake such other responsibilities and perform such other duties from time to time as may reasonably be required to meet the operating needs of *The Society*.
- In the discharge of such duties and the exercise of such powers, authority and discretion, conform to, observe and comply with the directions, restrictions, and regulations of *The Society*, made or given from time to time e.g. in the form of Chief Executive Officer Limitations policies.
- Comply with all legal requirements, statutory or otherwise, pertaining to the position and responsibility of the Chief Executive Officer.
- Faithfully serve *The Society*, and at all times use his/her best endeavours to promote its interest.

EIGHTH PART – Delegation to the Chief Executive Officer

- The Board delegates to the Chief Executive Officer responsibility for the implementation of its strategic direction/strategic plan, while complying with the Chief Executive Officer Delegation policies.
- Only the Board acting as a body can instruct the Chief Executive Officer. Typically all instruction to the Chief Executive Officer will be codified as policy.
- The Board will make clear *The Society*'s strategic direction, including performance indicators to be applied by the Board when reviewing *The Society*'s and the Chief Executive Officer's performance.
- The Board will make clear to the Chief Executive Officer, in writing, of any limitations or limits it chooses to place on his/her freedom to take actions or make decisions that the Board deems to be unacceptable within the delegation.
- The Chief Executive Officer is responsible for the employment, management and performance evaluation of all staff and volunteers employed/contracted to *The Society*.
- Neither the Board nor individual Board members will instruct staff or volunteers in any matters relating to their work.

- Provided that the Chief Executive Officer achieves the outcomes sought by the Board, and does so in a manner consistent with the Board's policies and *The Society*'s values, the Board will respect and support the Chief Executive Officer's choice of actions.
- The expert knowledge and experience of individual Board members are available to the Chief Executive Officer.

NINTH PART – Chief Executive Officer's Authority

Always with the proviso that the Chief Executive Officer's decisions be consistent with and not defeat the stated intent and spirit of the Board's policies, he/she is authorised to establish all operational policies, make all operational decisions and design, implement and manage all operational practices and activities.

Acknowledging a Board member's right to have access to any information necessary to meet his/her duty of care to *The Society*, the Chief Executive Officer may defer instructions or requests from individual Board members or from unofficial groups of Board members if, in his/her opinion, such requests or instructions are:

1. Inconsistent with the Board's policies;
2. Deemed to make unjustifiable intrusions into the Chief Executive Officer's or other volunteer or staff member's time; or
3. Unjustifiably costly to *The Society*.

TENTH PART – Chief Executive Officer Remuneration

- Chief Executive Officer remuneration will be decided by the Board as a body, based on terms and conditions that address *The Society* performance and executive market conditions.
- Organisational performance will be only that performance revealed by the monitoring system, to be directly related to criteria in policy that is given by the Board.
- Remuneration will cover the entire range of salary, compensation, benefits and all other forms.
- Remuneration will be competitive with similar performance within the marketplace, based on achievement of the Board's strategic direction and strategic goals while complying with the Executive Limitations Policies.
- A committee process will be used to gather information and provide options and recommendations for the Board, for its consideration and decision.

ELEVENTH PART – Chief Executive Officer
Performance Assessment

- The Chief Executive Officer's performance will be continuously, systematically and rigorously assessed by the Board against achievement of the Board-determined strategic outcomes and compliance with Chief Executive Officer Delegation policies.
- The Board will provide regular performance feedback to the Chief Executive Officer.
- The Board's assessment of the Chief Executive Officer's performance will be against only those performance indicators that have been agreed at the commencement of the performance year.
- The standard applied to all facets of the performance assessment shall be that the Chief Executive Officer has met, or can demonstrate compliance with, the intent or spirit of the Board policy/statement.
- The Board may monitor any policy at any time using any method, but will normally base its monitoring on a predetermined schedule.
- The Board may use any one or more of the following three methods to gather the information necessary to ensure Chief Executive Officer compliance with Board policies, and thus determine its satisfaction with that person's performance:

  1. Chief Executive Officer reporting;
  2. Advice from an independent, disinterested third party;
  3. Direct inspection by a Board approved Board member or group of Board members.

If at any time the Board engages an outside evaluator to assist in conducting an assessment of the Chief Executive Officer's performance, the process must be consistent with this policy. Any such evaluator is a contractor to the Board, not to the Chief Executive Officer.

TWELFTH PART – Chief Executive Officer
Delegation Policies

Overarching Chief Executive Officer limitations

The Chief Executive Officer must not take, allow or approve any action or circumstance in the name of *The Society* that is in breach of the law; is imprudent; contravenes any organisation specific or commonly held business or professional ethic; or is in breach of generally accepted accounting principles.

Financial planning

Budgeting/financial planning for any financial year or the remaining part of any financial year shall be designed to ensure the achievement of the Board-determined outcomes. In developing the operational financial plan and budget, and without limiting the scope of the foregoing, the Chief Executive Officer must not:

1. Fail to demonstrate a credible projection of revenues and expenses, a separation of capital and operational items, a projection of cash flows, or a disclosure of planning assumptions;
2. Create financial risk beyond Board-determined parameters;
3. Plan expenditure in any financial year that would result in default under any of *The Society*'s financing agreements or cause insolvency;
4. Fail to incorporate/accommodate medium to long-term financial plans/projections or long-term business direction;
5. Design a financial plan that anticipates the achievement of a 'bottom line' that is materially different from that determined by the Board, e.g. a predetermined surplus, acceptable deficit or balanced budget;
6. Fail to provide for the Board's developmental and other expenditures.

Financial management

The Chief Executive Officer is responsible for the day-to-day financial management of *The Society*. In carrying out this duty, he/she must ensure that nothing is done, or authorised to be done, that could in any way cause financial harm or threaten *The Society*'s financial integrity. Without limiting the scope of the foregoing, the Chief Executive Officer must not:

1. Use any organisational funds, enter into any contracts, nor accept any other liabilities, other than for the furtherance of Board-approved purposes and priorities;
2. Expend more funds than have been received in the financial year, unless offset by approved borrowings or approved withdrawals from reserves;
3. Allow undisputed invoices from suppliers of goods and services to remain unpaid beyond trade credit terms agreed upon with those suppliers;
4. Authorise expenditure beyond the level established by the Board;
5. Fail to meet all government imposed compliance requirements or payments on time and up to standard;
6. Breach accounting standards;
7. Acquire, encumber or dispose of land or buildings;

8. Neglect to ensure that there are limitations on expenditure and adequate controls on the use of credit or other purchase cards entrusted to card-holding staff or volunteers;
9. Fail to assertively pursue receivables overdue.

Investments

The Chief Executive Officer shall not allow or cause to allow *The Society*'s investment assets to be invested in a manner that threatens its financial security. Without limiting the scope of the foregoing, the Chief Executive Officer must not fail to maintain sufficient liquidity to meet short to medium-term financial commitments.

Remuneration and benefits

In managing the setting and review of salaries and benefits, the Chief Executive Officer must not:

1. Make decisions or promises that would in any way cause or threaten financial harm to *The Society*;
2. Change his/her remuneration;
3. Create obligations that cannot be met over the projected period of the individual's term of employment, or over a period for which revenues can realistically be projected;
4. Cause unfunded liabilities to occur, or in any way commit *The Society* to benefits that incur unpredictable future costs;
5. Make promises or guarantees of long-term employment when such guarantees or promises cannot realistically be honoured.

Protection of assets

The Chief Executive Officer shall not fail to take all prudent and reasonable actions to ensure that *The Society*'s assets, physical and intellectual, are protected against all foreseeable, damaging circumstances. Without limiting the scope of the foregoing, the Chief Executive Officer must not:

1. Permit any unauthorised person to handle cash;
2. Process the receipt or disbursement of funds outside of controls acceptable to the duly appointed auditor;
3. Allow assets to be insured for less than is considered necessary for prudent risk management;

4. Make any purchase of goods or services without protection against conflict of interest;
5. Fail to protect intellectual property, information or files from loss, improper use, improper purposes or significant damage;
6. Fail to ensure that there are appropriate and effective security systems in place to adequately safeguard against the loss, common damage or theft of staff, volunteer, customer or organisation property;
7. Fail to maintain a current assessment and evaluation of the risk factors that could conceivably disrupt *The Society*'s effective and efficient operation, nor fail to ensure that there are plans and systems that, should a crisis occur, will allow continuity of business.

Communication and support to the Board

The Chief Executive Officer shall not permit the Board to remain uninformed about issues and concerns essential to the meeting of its duty of care, the carrying out of its responsibilities and the meeting of its accountabilities to its owners and key stakeholders.

The Chief Executive Officer must not:

1. Neglect to provide, in a timely, accurate and understandable fashion, support and information addressing the various issues to be monitored by the Board;
2. Neglect to provide financial reports that make clear: significant trends, data relevant to agreed benchmarks and Board-agreed measures, and further Board financial data, as determined by the Board from time to time;
3. Fail to inform the Board of significant, external environmental trends, adverse media publicity, the achievement of – or progress towards the achievement of – the Board's strategic direction, or changes in the basic assumptions from which the Board's policies derive;
4. Fail to inform the Board when, for any reason, there is actual or anticipated noncompliance with a Board policy;
5. Neglect to inform the Board of any serious legal conflict or dispute, or any potentially serious legal conflict or dispute, that has arisen or might arise in relation to matters affecting *The Society*;
6. Fail to ensure that the Board is provided with the necessarily wide range of views and perspectives that support effective decision making;
7. Fail to bring to the Board's notice such occasions when it is in breach of its Board Processes policies, particularly when this relates to the Chief Executive Officer's ability to carry out his/her responsibilities;
8. Fail to deal with the Board as a whole, except when responding to individual requests for information or requests from Board committees or working parties.

Emergency Chief Executive Officer succession

The Board recognises that one of its major risks is the loss of key personnel, particularly its Chief Executive Officer. To this end, the Chief Executive Officer must not fail to ensure that there is in place an emergency management regime that can operate in the event of an unexpected loss of his/her services. There must also be at least one other person capable of responding to Board concerns and requirements at a level necessary for effective governance.

Employment conditions

In exercising the delegation of the management of staff and volunteers, the Chief Executive Officer must not fail to ensure that there is provided a workplace environment conducive to sound workplace practices, consistent with workplace legislation and *The Society*'s core corporate values.

The Chief Executive Officer must not:

1. Fail to provide staff and volunteers with clear guidelines as to their rights, entitlements and workplace obligations;
2. Fail to provide staff and volunteers with 'safe', 'dignified' and 'fair' working conditions, as defined in relevant workplace legislation;
3. Deny to any employees or volunteers their right to an approved and fair internal grievance process;
4. Refuse employee or volunteer access to the Board to express a grievance when
   o the internal grievance process has been properly followed;
   o the grievance asserts that the Chief Executive Officer has breached a Board policy to his/her detriment;
   o and/or the grievance asserts that the Board has not provided adequate protection of the volunteer's or staff member's human rights.

Where there is verifiable evidence of such a grievance, access to the Board is via the Chair. The Board reserves the right either to appoint an independent third party to mediate the matter, or to investigate and recommend an appropriate course of action itself, and must ensure that all staff or volunteer members are acquainted with their rights under this policy.

It is understood that, notwithstanding anything contained herein, the law is paramount. No principle stated here must be followed if it is contradicted by the law of jurisdiction.

Constitution 2: Constitution of a Public Entity

Name

The name of the entity is the Model Organisation (MO).

Interpretation

In this constitution

'Act' means the Associations Incorporation Act of 20** of the State of X as amended from time to time.

'Assurance Committee' means the persons nominated by the Minister to provide an oversight function to MO by providing members for the Board, as set out in the various sections.

'Authorised Signatories' means those members or employees of MO who are authorised by the Board to sign cheques and withdrawal forms on behalf of MO.

'Board' means the committee of management of MO.

'Chairman' or 'Chairperson' means the member appointed by the Minister to be Chairman of the Board.

'Customer Reference Group' means the customer reference group comprising of representatives from the departments and agencies of the government, or representing the same, as nominated by the Minister and providing members to the Board.

'DT Secretary' means the Secretary of the Department of Treasury.

'Executive Director' means the Executive Director of MO.

'Expert Reference Group' means the expert reference group comprising of technical experts from the departments and agencies of the government, or representing the same, as nominated by the Minister and providing members to the Board.

'Member' means a member of the Board of MO.

'Minister' means the Minister for State as the case may be.

'Minister's Delegate' means:

- the Department Secretary; or
- a person appointed by the Minister; or
- the holder of a position or office specified by the Minister, or representing the interests of the Minister, in relation to MO.

'Operational Management' includes financial management, provider and client relationship management, accommodation management services, and such other services as may be specified from time to time by the Minister or the Minister's Delegate.

'Quorum' is more than half the number of members.

'Regulations' means the Associations Incorporation Regulations.

'Secretary' means the person holding office under the Constitution as secretary of MO; or, where no such person holds office, the Public Officer of the association.

'Special Resolution' means a resolution passed by no less than three-quarters of the members that are present and entitled to vote at a meeting of the Board;

'MO Board Handbook' means the official handbook of the Board, as agreed upon and amended by members of MO from time to time.

Registered Office

The registered office of MO shall be 990 Bloggs St Metroville, BH3 123 or any other address notified to the Director-General from time to time.

Liability of Members

The members shall not be liable to contribute towards the payment of the debts and liabilities of MO.

Objects

The objects for which MO is established are to:

- Operate within the wider state government;
- Establish, implement and manage systems approved by the Minister (or the Minister's Delegate), including operational management;
- Establish the implementation of related projects as may be approved by the Minister; and
- Manage, administer and provide information about MO to the general public, including to particular interest and stakeholder groups.

Membership

Unless otherwise approved by the Minister:

- The Chairman and the members will be appointed by the Minister for a period of two years; and
- The Board will consist of a minimum of seven members and a maximum of thirteen members, including the Chairman. The members provided by the

Expert Reference Group, the Customer Reference Group and the Assurance Committee, respectively, shall be equal in number and no less than the minimum of 2 (in the case of a total of 7 members, including the Chairman), or more than the maximum of 4 (in the case of 13 members, including the Chairman).

A member (including the Chairman) shall cease to be a member:

- If that member dies, becomes insane, becomes bankrupt or, if an incorporated body, is wound up or dissolved;
- If that member, by notice in writing, resigns from membership of the Board;
- At the conclusion of the member's term of appointment; or
- If the Minister terminates that member's membership.

Role of the Chairman

The Chairman of the Board shall:

- Be the person appointed by the Minister;
- Undertake a public role in promoting an understanding of the work of MO;
- Act as the key spokesperson for MO;
- Advise the Minister on progress, as measured against MO's functions; and
- Consult the Minister (or the Minister's Delegate) in relation to decisions.

Role of Members

The members shall:

- Determine all matters relating to the operation of MO, noting clause X (Role of the Minister) and clause XX of the Constitution;
- Operate in accordance with the Role of Board Members and the Code of Conduct, outlined in the MO Board Handbook; and
- Appoint the Executive Director of MO.

Role of the Minister

The Chairman must seek approval from the Minister (or the Minister's Delegate) in relation to a decision that:

- Involves a significant change of policy for MO (other than a policy that only affects the internal operations of MO);
- Involves a significant change of strategic direction for MO; or
- May, in the Chairman's reasonable opinion, lead to significant political or media comment.

A decision referred to above does not take effect unless the Minister (or the Minister's Delegate) has approved the decision, in writing. The Minister (or the Minster's Delegate) must, after being advised of a decision, either approve, amend or reject the decision.

Decisions that involve a significant change of policy for MO include, but are not limited to, decisions relating to operational management.

The Minister (or Minister's Delegate) may, at any time, attend a meeting, or part of a meeting, of the Board.

If the Minister (or Minister's Delegate) attends a meeting, the Minister (or the Minister's Delegate) does so in the role of advisor and observer, and may not cast a vote on any motion before the Board.

Register of Members

The Public Officer of MO shall establish and maintain a register of members, specifying the name and address of each person who is a member, together with the date on which the person became a member.

The register of members shall be kept at the Principal Place of Administration of MO, and shall be open for inspection, free of charge, by any member at any reasonable hour.

Executive Director

The Executive Director shall carry out the following functions:

- Control and manage the day-to-day affairs of MO;
- Implement the decisions of the Board; and
- Carry out the functions given by the Chairman to perform on behalf of the Board or MO.

Public Officer

The Public Officer must be appointed by the Board in accordance with the Act.

Meetings

Meetings of the Board shall be called by the Chairman at least 6 times per year, and the Chairman shall, on the written request of a quorum of members, call a meeting to be held as soon as practicable, but no later than 21 days after the Chairman receives the request.

Subject to the Constitution, the place, date and hour of every meeting shall be determined by the Chairman; and written notice thereof, including the purpose of the meeting and the text of any Special Resolution intended to be proposed at the meeting, shall be given to the members and the Minister (or the Minister's Delegate) by any means the Chairman considers appropriate and, where a Special Resolution is to be proposed at that meeting, at least 21 days prior to the date of the meeting – or in any other case, at least seven days prior to the date of the meeting.

Any meeting papers provided to members for a meeting of the Board shall, at the same time, be provided to the Minister (or Minister's Delegate).

The Minister (or the Minister's Delegate) shall be advised of the annual Board meeting calendar. Where a meeting date or location has been changed, the Minister (or Minister's Delegate) shall be informed at least seven days prior to the meeting.

The secretary, or such person as the meeting appoints, shall keep proper minutes of the proceedings of all meetings.

No business shall be transacted at any meeting unless a quorum of members is present.

In the event that a member is not able to attend a meeting of the Board, that member shall not be able to appoint a proxy for the purposes of that meeting.

No other person shall attend a Board meeting without prior approval of the Chairman.

Decisions at any meeting of the Board shall be made by a majority of votes, and each member present shall have one vote. Voting shall be by show of hands unless the meeting decides otherwise. In the case of an equality of votes, the Chair of the meeting shall have a second or casting vote.

The Chairman shall be the Chair of all meetings at which he or she is present, but if he or she is not present, or does not wish to take the Chair, the members present shall elect a Chair for the meeting.

Consultants, Experts and Subcommittees

The Board may seek advice from individuals, and hire consultants with specific expertise to give advice to the Board. The Board may also establish committees, subject to such directions as the Board may give, to report to the Board on matters that further the objects of MO.

End of Financial Year

The financial year of MO shall commence on the first day of July each year and terminate on the 30th day of June in the following year.

Banking and Delegations

Official receipts shall be issued for all moneys received by MO.

All funds of MO shall, in the first instance, be deposited in a bank account of MO no later than the first working day following the day of receipt, or as soon as possible thereafter.

All cheques or withdrawals are to be signed by two authorised signatories.

Application of Funds and Property

All funds or property of MO not subject to any special trust shall be available, at the discretion of MO, for the purposes of carrying out the objects of MO, provided that no portion thereof shall be paid or applied directly or indirectly by way of dividend, bonus or otherwise howsoever to profit to any member, but nothing herein contained shall prevent the payment in good faith of reasonable and proper remuneration to any member, officer or employee of MO for, or in return for, services actually rendered to MO.

Accounts

Proper accounts and records of the transactions and affairs of MO shall be kept by the Executive Director. The Board shall do all things necessary to ensure all payments out of the moneys of MO are correctly made and properly authorised, and that adequate control is maintained over the assets of, or in the custody of, MO, and over the incurring of liabilities by MO.

All payments of moneys of MO shall be approved by the Board or, in the case of payments up to $60,000 – or up to $200,000 in the case of payroll payments, including Business Activity Statement payments – by the Executive Director.

The Board shall, as soon as practicable after each quarter of the financial year, cause to be prepared a report of the income and expenditure of MO for each quarter, and a balance sheet setting out the assets and liabilities of MO for each quarter.

Audit

The Board shall, as soon as practicable after an annual income and expenditure statement and a balance sheet have been prepared:

• Cause an auditor, registered as an auditor pursuant to the Corporations Act, to be appointed by the Board for the purpose of auditing the MO financial statements;

- Examine whether the income and expenditure statement and balance sheet are based on proper accounts and records, and are in agreement with those accounts and records; and
- Furnish a report of the results of the examination, drawing attention to any irregularities in the financial affairs of MO disclosed by the examination.

Alterations of Objects and the Constitution

The objects and Constitution of the MO may, subject to the prior written approval of the Minister, be altered by a resolution passed by a quorum of members. The proposed alterations must be specified in the notice of the meeting and forwarded to Board members at least 21 days prior to the date of an extraordinary meeting.

Winding Up

Despite anything in the Constitution, the MO may, subject to the prior written approval of the Minister, be altered by a resolution passed by a quorum of members. The proposed alterations must be specified in the notice of the meeting and forwarded to Board members at least 21 days prior to the date of an extraordinary meeting.

In the event of MO being wound up or dissolved, within 30 days of such winding up or dissolution:

- Any money (including interest on such money) or property received by MO from the commonwealth government that has not been applied, or that has been improperly applied, shall be repaid by MO to the government, and any assets of MO purchased with moneys received from the government must be returned to the government; and
- All other money or property received by MO that is not money or property referred must:
  1. Not be distributed to any member; and
  2. Be distributed to an institution, trust fund or organisation as determined by Special Resolution, having objects similar to the objects of MO, and prohibiting distribution of its income and property among its members to an extent at least as great as is imposed on MO.

Miscellaneous

Funds source:
The funds of MO shall be derived from the government and such other sources as the Board determines.

Inspection of books:

The records, books and other documents of MO shall be:

• Kept at the registered office of MO; and
• Open to inspection, free of charge, by members at any reasonable hour.

Resolution of internal disputes:

Where internal disputes cannot be resolved by the Chairman and members, disputes between members (in their capacity as members) of MO, and disputes between members and MO, are to be referred to a community justice centre for mediation in accordance with the Community Justice Centres Act.

At least 7 days before a mediation session is to commence, the parties are to exchange statements of the issues that are in dispute between them and supply copies to the mediator.

Constitution 3: Constitution of the Philatelic Society of Centralia

The function and purpose of the Philatelic Society of Centralia (*The Society*) is to foster the collection, study, scholarship and exchange of postage stamps from every country. It is a nonprofit organisation whose accounts are to be audited annually.

Address

The address of *The Society* shall be: PO Box 1234, Centralia. Tel. (09) 1234-5678; fax (09) 1234-9101. www.philatelic.org.

Meetings will be held in Room 21 of the Community Hall in Centralia, commencing at 7 pm and finishing no later than 9 pm on the advertised date.

The Committee

A committee shall be selected by a poll of all members, and by postal ballot.

It shall consist of no fewer than seven members and no more than nine.

The committee will, at its first meeting, elect a Chair from amongst its members.

There shall be a secretary, also elected from amongst its committee members at its first meeting.

There shall be a treasurer, also elected from amongst its committee members at its first meeting.

Each year there shall be a newly elected committee.

Candidates may stand more than once, but not more than once if there is a contender.

Having been out of office for a year, any member may stand again for the committee.

The committee may co-opt outside members for a particular purpose, but such co-opted members do not have a vote.

All committee members are to be delegates, and not to represent factional interests.

The committee shall have the power to disburse such funds as may be necessary in order to further the aims of *The Society*, subject to conventional audits.

Powers of the Committee

The task of the committee is to further the aims of *The Society* by such legal means as are available.

The powers of the committee and its office bearers are always subject to overriding law.

Committee members will fill their term of office, and may be dismissed only by a ballot of all members.

Frequency of Meetings

Meetings will be conducted no less than quarterly, with the fourth meeting of the year to be an AGM.

Notwithstanding the previous clause, any member seconded by another may cause a special meeting to be convened.

Quorum

A quorum shall be a majority of members physically present. Proxies do not count towards the quorum.

Calling a Meeting

A notice calling for agenda items is to be circulated at least two weeks before the meeting.

Meetings must be called by given written notice at least seven working days ahead of time.

Special meetings may be called at any time, provided each committee member is contacted personally by the secretary.

Motions

All substantive motions must be in the positive form.

Each substantive motion must have a proposer or seconder, or the motion lapses.

All procedural motions take precedence over substantive motions.

Rescission motions may be raised, but they may not be resolved until the next meeting, save exceptional circumstances or a unanimous vote of all members of the committee.

Voting

Voting shall be on a show of hands. Any member may require that such a vote be replaced by a secret written ballot.

Voting is to be decided according to first-past-the-post rules.

The Chair has a casting vote, which may be exercised at any time during the debate. It is understood that convention requires the casting vote to accord with the status quo unless there is good reason to the contrary.

Proxies

All proxies must be specific to the meeting in question, provided in writing by the donor and signed by him/her.

A proxy must be a member of *The Society*.

Proxies are there as delegates, not representatives.

Proxies do not count towards the quorum.

Declaration of Interest

Members who have a real or perceived conflict of interest must declare that interest, and must absent themselves from the room while the substantive issue is debated and resolved.

Recording of Committee Decisions

The secretary shall keep a record of decisions, and will prepare draft minutes for the committee to consider at its next meeting.

The minutes are not counted as a true record until the next meeting has ratified them as accurate. When so agreed, the Chair is to sign them as a true record.

The minutes of the previous meeting are to be put to motion as a true record, having had any issues resolved, and once passed are to be signed by the chairman as a true record.

Teleconferencing

Teleconferencing is not to be counted as a meeting unless agreed upon by all members of *The Society*.

AGENDAS

Examples of agendas follow. Readers should also note the principles outlined in Parts One and Two, which give advice about agendas in general. It should be appreciated that these proposals are subject to modification, legal requirements and the needs of the organisation. Readers will also note that sometimes the term *agendae* is used for the plural in other documents. This is a Latin derivative and not now in common use – indeed any current use is regarded as pretentious.

Agenda 1: Annual General Meeting of the International Society of Fumdumbulators

June 30th 2010
2.30 pm to 5.30 pm
Ground Floor
Council Chambers
1 Bloggs Street
Metropolis

Those present

Apologies

Declarations of conflict of interest

Starring of items

Call for items under 'any other business'

Approval of the previous minutes

Business arising from the minutes

Chairman's Report (attached)
  Motion: That the Chairman's Report be received

  Strategies for organisational growth and influence

  Discussion

Secretary's Report
  Motion: That the Secretary's Report be received

  Discussion

Treasurer's Report
  Motion: That the Treasurer's Report be received

  Motion: That a more detailed plan of expenditure be prepared in time for consideration at the next meeting

  Further discussion

Re. change of Code of Conduct
  Motion: That Section B(4) of the Code be amended to read:

  'That no research report be received or approved unless the research was first approved by the organisation's ethics committee'

Re. insurance
  It was noted that the organisation's insurance policy does not cover subcontractors.

  Motion: That every subcontractor to this organisation be required to produce documentary evidence of his/her insurance cover while working for this organisation.

Re. performance measures
  It was noted that each sector of the organisation works under the accountability model. As such, the criteria are as set out in the attached document.

Motion: That each sector of the organisation is to provide an annual accounting of performance to the supervisory head, and that the CEO and senior management give their accounting to the AGM.

Any other business

Date and time of next meeting
    30th June 2011: 2.30 to 5.30 pm. Venue to be advised.

Agenda 2: Meeting of the Faculty of Specialist Studies, University of Centralia

30th June 2008
Faculty Building
Main Campus
Room 210
2.00 pm to 4.30 pm

*Present
    Professor James Aloysius (Chairman)
    Mr Ross McIver MacDonald (Secretary)
    Dr David McLean
    Dr John Braven
    Ms Jean Simpson
    Mr Brett Dragan
    Dr Fiona McCampbell

*Apologies
    Dr Ingrid Norton Jones

*Proxy
    Dr David McLean has a written and signed proxy for Dr Jones

*Minutes of the previous meeting
    Motion: that they be accepted as a true record

*Business arising from the minutes

*Reconsideration of the policy of extensions for written work
    Motion: that the policy of requiring written work to be in on time be instated

Extensions are only to be granted where the Dean has approved them, and only then in exceptional circumstances.

*Approvals for the award of degrees
    Bachelor of Arts to be awarded to:
    Jean Carruthers Jones
    Michael John Howard
    William Hogget
    Dekin Weera Tussels
    Kerala Weerasekera
    Ian James Campbell

    Master of Arts to be awarded to:
    Colin Stewart Brown
    Barry James Smith
    Jean Hamilton Jones

*Policy on research ethics
    Motion: that every application for research ethics approval be submitted to the research ethics committee. Candidates may not declare their own research to be low risk, as the research ethics committee will decide the risk level.

*Additions to the committee
    It is recognised that expertise is needed for next year's meetings on the subject of the economics of research grant applications (Dr Finlay's CV is attached).

    Motion: that the committee approve Dr Cameron Finlay as an observer and advisory member of the committee for the year 2009.

*Any other business

*Date and time of next meeting
    30th September 2008. Venue to be advised in the minutes.

(It is to be noted that the items starred above are always to be starred. The unstarred items may be accepted *en bloc*, but any member may star any item, which will then be discussed. That starring may be for reasons as detailed as those applying to (say) a candidate for graduation.)

MINUTES

Preliminary Comment

The word 'minute' has several connotations. It can mean to make a quick note (done in a minute). It can also mean a rough draft of a document, or a memorandum. In the present context, the minutes (short for 'minutes of a meeting') are an official record of the proceedings and decisions.

Minutes 1 – *Proforma* Minute Structure: Minutes of the Meeting of the XXX Board

Held on _____

At _____

Commencing at _____

PRESENT

_____

_____

_____

_____

APOLOGIES

_____

_____

_____

There were no declarations of interest.

1. WELCOME AND APOLOGIES

    The Chairman welcomed all members and declared the meeting open. He asked members for any items of general business for notification and inclusion in General Business.

2. MINUTES OF THE PREVIOUS MEETING

    MOVED _____ SECONDED _____

    THAT the minutes of the meeting held on the _____ be approved as a true and correct record.

    CARRIED

3. MATTERS ARISING FROM THE MINUTES

    All matters arising from the minutes were discussed under individual headings.

4. ISSUES FOR DISCUSSION
   4.1. _____
   The Chairman tabled _____ paper on _____
   MOVED _____ SECONDED _____
   CARRIED <u>Action</u>:

5. REPORTS
   5.1   To consider draft Strategic Plan
   MOVED _____ SECONDED _____
   THAT_____
   CARRIED <u>Action</u>:

6. FINANCE
   6.1. To consider planned budget and results against SSP performance
         indicators.
   MOVED _____ SECONDED _____
   CARRIED <u>Action</u>:

   6.2. To appoint the External Auditor
   MOVED_____ SECONDED _____
   CARRIED <u>Action</u>:

   6.3. Approval of the Financial Report
   MOVED _____ SECONDED _____
   THAT the financial report be accepted.
   CARRIED <u>Action</u>:

   NEXT MEETING
   The next meeting of the _____ will be held on _____.
   There being no further business, the Chairman thanked all members for
   attending and declared the meeting closed at _____.

   Signed as a true and correct record.

   _____   _____
   CHAIRMAN   DATE

Minutes 2: Minutes of the AGM of a Cluster Village

Held at 99 Old York Street
Brightown

Body Corporate number 1234

Wednesday, September 23rd 2009

MINUTES

Present: John Brown (Chair), Rosemary Smith (Secretary), Gertrude
            Carruthers, Ian J. Maloof, James Andrews
Apology: Jean Jones

Minutes of last meeting: The minutes of the meeting held on 30th March 2009 were confirmed

Business arising from the 2008 AGM:

1. Insurance:
    Rosemary Smith to look into Pay Happy Insurance Company, and compare it with Costless Insurance Company. To compare what is covered, reputation, and value for money.

2. Reflectors: for driveway entrance
    Ian J. Maloof to arrange to have driveway reflectors installed to facilitate entry at night.

3. Blocked drain: from the intersection of Alpha and Omega streets
    Local government has a plan to fix the drainage problems at the bottom of the property. This item to be retained for the next agenda.

    It was noted that an abandoned car has been removed from outside of the rear of the property.

4. Nuisance tree: from outside unit number 10; seems to be dead
    Fiona to establish whether it is on private or Body Corporate land, with a view to its removal.

General Business:

1. Parking and letter to the Council:
   The Council rejected requests that the parking spaces opposite our exit drive be cancelled and a no-parking sign erected. This would have enabled local council trucks to turn in and out of the property more easily. It was noted that the Council declined, but did agree to widen the concrete entrance to our private road.

2. Body Corporate Green Bin:
   The Body Corporate Green Bin at the end of the driveway has been rented to save the BC's gardeners' tipping fees, and is working well so far. The bin is not for general use.

3. Grounds report:
   Gertrude and the gardener have attended to the spiking of the ground and watering of Saturade around the elm tree in Centre Park.

   Jean has painted our street number on the kerb, using luminous paint.

   John and James have been liaising successfully with the local government drainage department. The outcome is that parking places opposite our entrance road are to be removed, so that turning into our private roadway is made easier.

Welcome:
   A warm welcome is extended to Bruce and Betty McGregor, who have moved into unit 21.

   Motion: that a letter of welcome be sent to the McGregors, welcoming them to the complex and inviting them to attend any Body Corporate committee that they might wish.

Next Meeting:
   Thursday 9th September 2010
   99 York Street
   Brightown
   4.00–6.30 pm

USEFUL CHECKLISTS

What follows are checklists for various listed items.

This section contains several example documents. As before, they are to be viewed as instances rather than infallible examples. As such, they are to be seen as starting points and indicators. The documents are, respectively, (1) Conflict of Interest; (2) The Public Entity: Directors' Code of Conduct; (3) Resolution Summary Sheet; (4) Summary of Meeting Procedures; and (5) Declaration of Relevant Personal Details.

These sheets should be seen as guides. They will, it is hoped, form a point of departure and a guide for an organisation to develop its own guide sheets.

Conflict of Interest

Use this at each committee or board meeting.

❑ Following the opening of the meeting, ask all members to declare any potential conflict of interest arising out of any issues to be put to the meeting.
Record response
Name of member
Issue of conflict _____

❑ Note the disclosure of the conflict of interest and the decision of the committee or board on how to deal with this conflict.
Record response

❑ Confirm that, if a conflict of interest exists that provides a financial benefit to a member, that the named member will refrain from voting, and will absent him/herself from the meeting while the substantive issue is debated and resolved.

❑ Ensure that the minutes record the declaration of interests declared at this meeting.
Record response

Dated the _____ day of _____ 20____

The Public Entity: Directors' Code of Conduct

This code identifies the following duties for members of public sector boards. These are also found in the various state-owned enterprises acts and corporations law acts.

Duty	Guidelines
Act with honesty and integrity	Be open and transparent in your dealings; Use power responsibly; Do not place yourself in a position of conflict of interest; Strive to earn and sustain public trust of a high level.
Act in good faith in the best interests of the public entity	Demonstrate accountability for your actions; Accept responsibility for your decisions; Do not engage in activities that may bring you or the public entity into disrepute.
Act fairly and impartially	Avoid bias, discrimination, caprice or self-interest; Demonstrate respect for others by acting in a professional and courteous manner.
Use information appropriately	Ensure information gained as a director is only applied to proper purposes and is kept confidential.
Use your position appropriately	Do not use your position as a director to: Seek an undue advantage for yourself, family members or associates; Cause detriment to the public entity. Ensure that you decline gifts or favours that may cast doubt on your ability to apply independent judgement as a board member of the public entity.
Act in a financially responsible manner	Understand financial reports, audit reports and other financial material that comes before the board; Actively inquire into this material.
Exercise due care, diligence and skill	Ascertain all relevant information; Make reasonable enquiries; Understand the financial, strategic and other implications of decisions.
Comply with the establishing legislation, or its equivalent, for your public entity	Act within the powers and for the functions set out in your public entity's establishing legislation and/or ministerial charter.
Demonstrate leadership and stewardship	Promote and support the application of the Victorian public sector values; Act in accordance with the Directors' Code.

Resolution Summary Sheet

CHAIR _____

BOARD MEETING NO. _____ DATE _____

Resolutions passed at the meeting	Action required	Time of completion	Person responsible
1.			
2.			
3.			
4.			
5.			
6.			
7.			
8.			
9.			
10.			

COMMENTS:

Filed in resolution records   Date / /

Summary of Meeting Procedures

Table of proposed issues

Calling members' meetings	The Chair may at any time convene a meeting, but must do so when requested by any member and a seconder.
Chairing members' meetings	The Chair or, in his/her absence, the deputy Chair, or, in the absence of both, a member appointed by the board.
Quorum at members' meetings	The quorum is a majority of members who must be physically present throughout the meeting.
A proxy	A member may (or may not) appoint a proxy to attend a meeting.
Passing of members' resolutions	A resolution is passed by a majority of members' votes; the Chair has a casting vote, which may be exercised at any time during the debate.
How voting is carried out	Voting may be by a show of hands unless a poll is demanded any member.
Circulating resolutions	The members can pass a resolution without a meeting if all members sign a statement of agreement with the resolution.
Timing of meetings	The board must meet at least six times in each calendar year, and at least once every three months.
Minister (political)	The minister (or the minister's delegate) may attend meetings, but may not vote on any motion.
Notice to members	Notice is to be given by post at least seven working days prior to the date of the meeting.
When notice by email or fax is given	A notice by fax or electronic means is deemed to be sufficient if it is 'read' three working days prior to the meeting.
Notice of adjourned meetings	If a meeting is adjourned for one month or more, a notice of a new meeting must be issued.
Business at adjourned meetings	Only unfinished business may be transacted on resumption after an adjournment.
Methods of communication	If a majority of members agree, a meeting of the board or its committees may be held by means of alternative methods of communication, or a combination of methods.

Declaration of Personal Details

The secretary shall establish and maintain:

(1) A register of members, specifying the name and address of each person who is a member, together with the date on which the person became a member;

(2) A register of relevant interests, which contains any details of the nature and extent of a member's interests in shares in companies; any details or instructions that a member has given about the acquisition or disposal of shares; and any details of offices held in other companies or government entities.

NAME

ADDRESS

TELEPHONE

EMAIL

Registrable interests during the return period	Details
1. The income source of any financial benefit you received or are entitled to receive.	
2. The name of any company or other body in which you held office as a member or otherwise.	
3. The name or description of any company or other body in which you hold a beneficial interest.	
4. Whether you hold memberships in other organisations that may compete with your present appointment as a member.	
5. A concise description of any trust of which you or a member of your family are a trustee, or of which you or a member of your family hold a beneficial interest, that also does business with the present committee or board.	
6. The address or description of any land within which you hold beneficial interest that the present committee or board is likely to own or use.	
7. The above applies to any relatives or those with whom you live.	

Part Five

THE FORMAL RULES

A: Useful Definitions

In order for meetings to run successfully, they need to be bound by common rules, and to work according to agreed definitions. To that end, a few useful definitions are given here.

Attendance
> For a member to remain on a committee or board, there should be a requirement of a minimum of attendance in person (say, 75 per cent). Where such attendance requirements are not met, then the member is removed from membership and replaced. When so removed from membership, the person who failed to attend is disbarred from being eligible for membership again until the next election or appointment.

> The giving of a proxy constitutes an attendance, save a personal presence is required for at least 50 per cent of meetings.

Base motives
> It should be an assumption in meetings that all members act from good motives. The misattribution of morally dubious motives should be subject to censure.

Conflict of interest
> A conflict of interest occurs when a fact, perception, or belief compromises professional objectivity.

Consensus
> Consensus is an informal agreement as to decisions. The Chair may express the view that there is consensus over a particular motion, but that is a challengeable assumption.

Courtesy
> Courtesy is the application of the rules of civilised behaviour that govern personal interchange. It is based upon the assumption that all people are

dignified entities deserving of respect. It involves the attributes of good motives and goodwill.

Delegate and representative

The critical distinction is that delegates have powers delegated to them to endorse such decisions as seem reasonable in the light of the discussion. Representatives represent a particular set of interests, and will vote according to the views they represent.

Majority

A majority vote means the number of votes (including proxies) rather than the number of members present.

Mindset

At worst, mindset is an attitude in which a particular orientation is taken and preserved, and which may interfere with rational functioning; at best, it is a view that goodwill and reason will prevail, as will the rules of civilised debate.

Minutes

Minutes are a written record of what was done and what was agreed upon at the previous meeting. The existence of minutes ensures that there are no problems of differential recollection. It also ensures, by confirmation of the minutes, that certain items were resolved and to be acted on.

The acceptance of the minutes is just that. They are not debated unless there is an omission or an inaccuracy. Any subsequent discussion is addressed as 'business arising from the minutes'.

Procedural motions

A procedural motion is one that relates to the conduct and procedures of the meeting alone, and is not a substantive motion (e.g. 'That the speaker is not addressing the motion that is being debated', or 'That the motion now be put').

Proxy

A proxy is a voting stand-in for a member who is not able to attend. The proxy bearer will ensure that a signed and dated letter conferring the proxy is given to the secretary.

The constitution will state whether or not a proxy must be another member of that committee.

When members are voting, they must indicate that they are voting in their own right, and must also indicate when they are proxy voting on another's behalf. It is conceivable that that a member could vote one way for him/herself, and be directed to vote in the opposite way by the person represented by proxy. It is essential to make sure the Chair is aware of which vote is being exercised.

Questions

Where a member asks a question of any other member of the committee or the organisation that is pertinent to the committee's deliberations, such a question must be answered to the questioner's satisfaction.

Quorum

The minimum number of attendees required for a passed motion to be adopted. This definition should include the notion that a valid, written, and signed proxy is equivalent to attendance.

Regular meetings and special meetings

A regular meeting is one that is scheduled, such as an annual general meeting (AGM) or a monthly meeting. A special meeting is one that is called for a particular purpose or particular reason. An example of a special meeting is an extraordinary general meeting (EGM), or a meeting to address a particular crisis.

Rescission motion

This is a substantive motion to rescind a previous decision of a committee or board, commonly given on notice, and to be resolved at the next meeting.

Rules of debate

The set of agreed procedures by which meetings will be conducted.

Substantive motions: Notices of motion

A substantive motion is one that has substance and leads to a particular external outcome (e.g. 'That all Directors shall receive an annual fee that is equal to one half of the average wage within the company', or 'That a letter of thanks be sent to Ms X, recognising her great contribution to the committee over a period of 25 years').

It is noted that procedural motions take precedence over substantive motions because they affect the course of the meeting and the processes by which decisions are reached.

Readers should appreciate that this list is an example. It may well be that particular committee and boards need to define other terms, or redefine these. It is worth recording that such defining must precede particular cases. The reason for defining before a particular triggering event is that one is then assured that the principle was not made to fit the case, but rather the principle is superordinate to any particular case, thus ensuring fairness.

B: The Constitution

For a meeting to be properly constituted, there needs to be a constitution which sets out the purpose, functions, and powers of the committee or board. The constitution is the basic frame of reference for the committee, and governs not only what it may do or not do, but also how it is constituted, and how it proceeds.

The constitution of a committee sets out the committee's purpose, powers and limitations, and defines the committee's role and the conduct of meetings.

Among the inclusion for mention are:

- The powers of the committee and its office bearers (always subject to overriding law, for the committee should not, and may not, act beyond its powers), and the rights and obligations of office bearers and members The size of the committee
- The election of the committee
- How office bearers are chosen
- All terms of office
- How any office bearer or committee member is dismissed if necessary
- Which office bearers there are to be (commonly a Chair, a Deputy Chair, a secretary, and a treasurer)
- The frequency of meetings
- Allowances for any special meetings if needed
- The committee's powers of co-option
- Whether co-opted members have voting rights
- That all committee members are to be delegates, and not represent factional interests
- The definition of a quorum, and specifically on which special occasions a larger quorum is required
- How voting is to be conducted (by voice, show of hands, secret ballot, etc.)
- How votes are to be counted (first-past-the-post, preferential, etc.)
- The conditions of a Chair's vote, particularly the casting vote

- The format/presentation/manner/submission of proxies (specifically that they must be written and signed by the giver of the proxy)
- Whether a proxy-carrying person is permitted to be present with a proxy vote if s/he is not a member of the committee or board
- That proxy votes count as a vote as though the person was present
- Whether a proxy counts towards a quorum
- Declarations of conflict of interest
- A prescription concerning rescission motions
- What notice is to be given calling for agenda items
- How notice of meetings is to be delivered, and the lead time required What the minutes record (e.g. fixed items, motions passed, whether who proposed a motion is recorded, etc.)
- That the minutes of the previous meeting are to be put to motion as a true record, any issues resolved, and signed by the Chair as a true record

It is recognised that video conferencing is likely to become more common, but that should not negate the points made above. Any extra considerations that might be necessary for video conferencing should be in addition to the general guides. Such guides might include items such as whether or not the video also records, and under what conditions of protection.

No voting member of the committee shall be present if s/he has a conflict of interest. If there is any potential for such a conflict of interest, the member shall declare it and absent him/herself from the meeting while the issue is debated and resolved. That may apply to board–management separation. In all of this, the principle of natural justice should apply.

C: Formal Processes

Meeting time and place
Members shall be notified of the meeting in accordance with the provisions of the constitution. It shall be with due notice in writing, posted and advertised according to agreed rules. It shall state the place of the meeting, the starting time and the latest finishing time.

Failure to hold a meeting
Suppose that a meeting is to be convened and, for some reason, is not held. Here the intent and circumstances are critical. With good intent, and for good reason, one occasionally hears of meetings that are convened but not held. In such circumstances the meeting is reconvened, and no damage done. If, on the other hand, a meeting is not held for some subversive reason, or not held out of pique or ill will, then members must insist that it be held.

When a meeting is being held and the Chair cannot stay, it is not proper that the meeting be terminated. The proper course of action is to appoint a new Chair or an interim Chair. No Chair is so indispensable that a meeting cannot be held if s/he is either absent or has to leave early; it is up to the meeting to decide.

The agenda

The agenda has some informal aspects to it. Agendas must have some structure, but there is still room for manoeuvre. The opening part, for example, is fixed (those present, proxies, consideration of the minutes of the previous meeting (including any amendments and subsequent approval as a true record), business arising, etc.). The end of the meeting has any other business, and the date, time and place of the next meeting. Within that, it is possible to structure the agenda in such a way as to put like items together.

Since meetings involve many people with busy schedules, it is necessary to state the time and place of the meeting, and the latest finishing time. Mention might also be made of the maximum time that may be allotted to any agenda item – always at the Chair's discretion. This may also be governed by the setting of agreed time limits to speeches, as is done in many legislatures.

Order of business

Items of business to be dealt with at a meeting should appear on the agenda in a regular order. A fairly common order is:

- Calling of the meeting to order and announcement of the opening of formalities
- Recording of who is present, and acceptance of apologies
- Notice and acceptance of proxies
- Record of previous meeting minutes, amendments and approval.
- Business arising from the minutes
- Agreement on the Agenda
- Calls for starring of items
- Acceptance of all unstarred items
- Substantive items dealt with seriatim
- Any other business
- Close of meeting with date set for next meeting

(See example of Agendas)

The minutes of the previous meeting are put up for approval and/or amendment, followed by business arising. This is followed by the set of substantive motions, any other business, the determination of date of next meeting and, finally, closure of meeting.

Proxies

The Chair shall call for all proxies to be recorded. All proxies must be in writing and signed by the person giving the proxy.

Quorum

A quorum is the minimum number of members required to be present before any business can be conducted. Unless otherwise specified, it is usually accepted that a simple majority of members entitled to vote constitutes a quorum.

One exception may be that certain classes of motion may require a larger than usual majority – for example, a move to change the constitution, which may require, say, 75 per cent of members present. These special conditions should be specified in the constitution.

The most notable exception to the simple-majority quorum is in legislatures. Because a number of legislative members may, for good reason, be absent for a debate, a quorum may be a lesser number (such as one-quarter or one-fifth of members).

The constitution should note whether or not the recording of a proxy constitutes an attendance.

Starring items

The agenda will include the required items for discussion to be starred, which will then be addressed by the meeting. Any member may call for any other items to be starred. When the committee is satisfied that all required items are starred, then a motion may be taken that all unstarred items be approved. If carried, that motion disposes of all of the noncontroversial items.

Treating linked proposals *en bloc*

Sometimes there are proposals that are so linked that it could be possible to treat them *en bloc*. In such circumstances, the items might be starred so that if any member wishes to object to a particular motion s/he may do so. If there is no objection to bloc treatment, it is a way of advancing through business in a rapid but seemly manner.

D: Committee Roles

Election of Chair and Deputy Chair

A Chair and Deputy Chair should be elected according to the prescriptions of the constitution. The Chair is responsible for running the meeting, and the secretary for recording the minutes. The Chair and secretary will, in consultation, call for and receive agenda items, arrange the agenda, and ensure that all members are notified of it.

The Chair is responsible for guiding the meeting through the agenda, ensuring that the rules of procedure are followed, and preserving order. The Chair's general responsibility is to ensure that the views of members are adequately expressed, and that any resolution reached by the meeting represents a decision in accordance with the rules of the constitution.

The Chair is entitled to the respect of members, and commonly not subjected to a vote of no confidence. If the Chair's conduct of a meeting is unsatisfactory to a majority of members, a motion, 'That X take the Chair for the remainder of the meeting', may be introduced, debated and voted upon. This motion has the status of a point of order and must be accepted immediately by the Chair. If the Chair is vacated for any other reason, the meeting is closed, save that an interim Chair be appointed.

Challenge to the Chair

If and when a challenge is made to the chairship, then there are options available. These include a member framing a procedural motion 'That X take the chairship of this meeting'. Other options include suspending standing orders, adjourning the meeting, or cancelling the meeting until the issue is resolved (see Part One for further comment).

Election of a secretary

The secretary is responsible for compliance with the constitution and the general rules of calling and recording a meeting. The records (i.e. the minutes) must record date and place of meeting, names of those present, and all resolutions passed at the meeting. It is common practice is to record the motions passed, but to omit discussion. The minutes have no standing as a record of the meeting until confirmed by members at the next meeting.

Where extra information is required for any item, or where a co-opted member is required, the Chair and secretary will arrange such conditions, and ensure that the rules of co-option and presentation are observed.

Right to speak

All members of the committee have the right to speak on any item, and should be encouraged to do so by the Chair. All voting members have the right to raise procedural matters during a meeting, and to vote. All voting members have the right to know any information relevant to the deliberations on any substantive motion. All co-opted members may have the right to speak at the meeting, at the invitation of the Chair, but shall not be allowed to vote. These same strictures apply to any other person present (such as an observer).

Interruptions of speakers should only occur where there is a point of order: a calling on a quorum or a move to closure, or a motion 'that the speaker no longer be heard' or 'that strangers be excluded'.

Right to propose and second motions

A member of a meeting has the right to propose and second motions, engage in debate, and vote. In some cases, a category of nonvoting members exists. Such members are usually permitted to engage in debate and raise points of order, but are not permitted to propose or second business motions, or to vote. All persons present at a meeting are entitled to an equal opportunity to contribute to debate, and to protection against abuse, defamatory statements, imputations of improper motives and allegations of improper conduct.

There are occasions in debate when it is appropriate to foreshadow a motion, *such as when* the foreshadowed motion is both relevant to what is to be determined by the motion that is on the table, and when the foreshadowed motion can help members make up their minds.

Orderly conduct

All persons present at a meeting are expected to observe the rules of procedure, and conduct themselves in an orderly manner. They must observe the authority of the Chair.

Recording dissent

Every member who is entitled to vote has the right to have his or her dissent from a decision of the meeting recorded in the minutes. If a member disagrees strongly with a motion that has been passed, his or her dissent can be recorded in the minutes so that later s/he cannot be accused of supporting a motion at odds with his or her conscience.

E: Procedural Matters

Order of procedure

All meetings shall follow the order of procedure required by the constitution, or by prior agreement if the constitution is silent on the matter.

Calling to order

Every meeting shall begin by calling the meeting to order, thereby noting that the formal meeting has started, and procedure is to be followed.

Agreement on the agenda

The Chair shall call for agreement about the agenda, and ask if any member wishes to propose any items under the agenda heading 'Any other business'.

Starring of items

All starred items must be discussed. The essential starred items are: those present, proxies, adoption of the minutes of the previous meeting, and time and date of next meeting.

All of the rest of the items may be unstarred. The Chair then asks if any member wishes to have an item starred. Any member may have any item starred.

The Chair may ask for a motion that all the unstarred items be adopted. If that is passed, then all of the unstarred items are then considered to be passed.

Starring is useful where there is a long list, much of which is not contentious. For example, in a university meeting there might be long list of those eligible to be awarded a degree. Any particular case might be starred for discussion (perhaps because of a clerical mistake or error of fact). Only that starred item will be discussed, and all others passed by the general motion of adopting unstarred items.

Motions

All business should be dealt with by motion, each motion to be proposed and seconded; any motion that does not find a seconder thereby lapses.

The proposer is invited to speak first, then the Chair invites other members to speak. This usually gives rise to a debate of 'for' and 'against'. When the debate has been concluded, the Chair puts the motion. Provided there is a quorum and the requisite number of votes, the motion is then determined.

Amendments to motions

From the discussion it may emerge that the motion would be more acceptable if it were amended. The Chair then invites someone to propose an amendment. An amendment must be introduced before the original motion is put to a vote, and must be in the spirit of the original motion. It must not negate or nullify the original motion.

Motions must not only be clear but also unambiguous. For example, 'that John Brown be appointed as Chair', rather than 'John Brown be nominated as Chair'. The latter is merely a nomination, whereas the former is clearly intended to have a practical outcome.

An amendment takes precedence over the original motion and, if carried, becomes the motion before the Chair. Amendments to motions must be acceptable to the mover and seconder.

That amendment is then put; if carried, the next motion is that the amended motion becomes the substantive motion, and debate then ensues, culminating in the amended motion being put.

The form of motions

All motions must be of a kind that is affirmative; the point here is that motions must be specific and leave no doubt about the intent. For example, the motion that board members have their stipend increased by 10 per cent is clear; the motion that board members are not to have their stipend increased by 10 per cent is ambiguous. (Up to 20 per cent? Decreased by 10 per cent? Left unchanged?)

Motion to rescind (rescission motions)

A motion to rescind a decision of the meeting requires at least the same rules as those of other substantive motions.

Unless the matter is very urgent, it is prudent to have a rescission motion deferred until the next meeting.

As rescission motions are usually contentious, it is important to have the rules governing such motions prescribed by the constitution. It is not generally accepted at the meeting that made the decision in question. Notice of such a motion, to be introduced at a subsequent meeting, is usually required; they are called 'rescission motions'. Notwithstanding, it is important to note that there should be a firm guideline that deals with rescission motions.

Procedural motions (points of order)

Meetings proceed by way of substantive motions; such motions are, as the name implies, matters of substance (for example, that the board approves the accounts). The other kind of motion is a procedural one.

A procedural motion is one that refers specifically to the way that a substantive motion is being dealt with. Examples of procedural motions are that:

- The speaker is not addressing the substantive motion under discussion
- The debate be adjourned to a future date
- A motion to adjourn a meeting must specify the date and time to which the meeting is to adjourn.
- At the time that an adjourned meeting resumes, it completes the original agenda, and does not deal with new matters.
- A speaker has improperly imputed improper motives to another member of the committee
- The motion be put (where debate has gone on too long)
- There is an unauthorised departure from the rules of procedure
- The Chair has ruled on a matter which a member wishes to dissent (in such a case, another member should be elected to chair until the dissent has been resolved)
- A member wishes to record his/her dissent from a passed motion
- Standing orders be suspended
- The meeting be adjourned

Note:
In order for a meeting to proceed in an orderly way, a procedural motion always takes precedence over a substantive motion.

Suspended meetings and suspended standing orders

A meeting may be suspended for an agreed reason, and for a short period.

Sometimes this suspension will take the form of suspension of standing orders. The suspension of standing orders means that the formal rules of debate are not in operation. This is commonly done where an issue is contentious and someone wishes the heat to die down – often a refreshment break is an appropriate means of proceeding. When a suitable short period has elapsed, the Chair will again call the meeting to order.

Adjourned meetings

Where it is agreed that a meeting be adjourned, then the resumption of the meeting at a future date will follow, during which the original agenda will be completed; it is not a new meeting with new items.

F: Issues Arising

Common problems arise in meetings. Among them are:

- Depending on the purpose of the committee and its constitution, it may be appropriate to adopt the Chatham House Rule.
- Motions from the Chair do require a seconder. This convention may be breached on grounds of courtesy where a Chair might, for example, propose a vote of thanks to an outgoing member.
- Reports should be dealt with by motion (for example, 'that report X be received'). After the motion is passed, the Chair invites comments on the report.
- Excessive formality is not always necessary. Thus a Chair may use an expression such as 'If there is no objection'.
- Suspension of standing orders allows a free discussion, unfettered by the rules of meetings. This may take one of two forms: one for a free debate on a contentious issue, the other for a relaxed discussion with freedom of expression.
- A motion to rescind is preferably dealt with at the next meeting, as the lapse of time permits reflection, and may be used for lobbying.
- Where there is a motion to adjourn a meeting, the date and time of resumption should be specified.

REFERENCES

Adair, J. 1984. *Training for Communication*. Aldershot: Gower.

Ardrey, R. 1966. *The Territorial Imperative*. New York: Athenaeum.

Argyle, M. 1988. *Bodily Communication*. London: Routledge.

Argyris, C. 1999. *On Organizational Learning*, 2nd ed. Oxford: Blackwell.

Armstrong, A. 2004. 'Measuring the effectiveness of corporate governance standards'. In A. Armstrong and R. Francis (eds), *Applications of Corporate Governance*, 55–61. Sydney: Standards Australia International.

Armstrong, A. and R. Francis (eds). 2004a. *An Introduction to Corporate Governance*. Sydney: Standards Australia International.

———— (eds). 2004b. *Applications of Corporate Governance*. Sydney: Standards Australia International.

Armstrong, A. and Z. Unger. 2009. 'Assessment, evaluation and improvement of university council performance'. *Evaluation Journal of Australasia* 9 (1): 46–54.

Asprey, M. 2010. *Plain Language for Lawyers*. Annandale: Federation Press.

Australian Corporations and Securities Legislation. 2001 Corporations Law. Sydney: CCH Australia Ltd.

Axtell, R. E. 1998. *Gestures: The Do's and Taboos of Body Language around the World*. New York: Wiley.

————· 1999. *Do's and Taboos of Humor around the World*. New York: Wiley.

Ayres, I. 2007. *Super Crunchers*. London: John Murray.

Bales, R. F. 1970. *Personality and Interpersonal Behaviour*. New York: Holt, Rhinehart & Winston.

————· 2009. 'The equilibrium problem in small groups'. In M. Argyle (ed.), *Social Encounters*, 221–36. London: Aldine Transaction.

Beatty, D. R. 2010. 'Practical tips for keeping strategy at the top of the agenda'. *Inside AICD*. Sydney: Australian Institute of Company Directors.

Belbin, M. 1993a. *Management Teams: Why They Succeed or Fail*. Oxford: Butterworth-Heinemann.

————· 1993b. *Team Roles at Work*. Oxford: Butterworth-Heinemann.

Bell, L. C. 2002. 'Senatorial discourtesy: The Senate's use of delay to shape the federal judiciary'. *Political Research Quarterly* 55 (3): 589–607.

Bion, W. R. 1961. *Experiences in Groups*. London: Tavistock.

Bolman, L. G. and T. E. Deal. 1991. *Reframing Organisations: Artistry, Choice and Leadership*. San Francisco: Jossey-Bass.

Branscombe, N. R. and B. Doosje. 2004. *Collective Guilt: International Perspectives*. Cambridge: Cambridge University Press.

Bull, P. 2001. 'State of the art: Nonverbal communication'. *The Psychologist* 14 (12): 644–7.

Carter, D. A, B. J. Simkins and G. Simpson. 2003. 'Corporate governance, board diversity, and firm value'. *Financial Review* 38 (1): 33–53.

Carver, J. 1997. *Boards That Make a Difference: A New Design for Leadership in Nonprofit and Public Organizations*. San Francisco: Jossey-Bass.

Chase, W. P. 1953. 'Principles of human relations, applications to management'. *Journal of Applied Psychology* 37 (5): 432–3.

Chen, E. T. and J. Nowland. 2010. 'Optimal monitoring in family-owned companies? Evidence from Asia'. *Corporate Governance: An International Review* 18 (1): 3–17.

Clark, J. 2005. *Working with Monsters*. Milsons Point, Australia: Random House Australia.

Clarke, T. E. 2004. *Theories of Corporate Governance*. New York: Routledge

Coles, J. L, N. D. Daniel and L. Naveen. 2008. 'Boards: Does one size fit all?' *Journal of Financial Economics* 87 (2): 329–56.

Collins, J. 2001. 'Level 5 leadership: The triumph of humility and fierce resolve'. *Harvard Business Review* 79 (1): 67–76.

Compton, W. C. 2005. *An Introduction to Positive Psychology*. Belmont, CA: Thomson-Wadsworth.

Covey, S. R. 2004. *The 7 Habits of Highly Effective People: Restoring The Character Ethic*. New York: Free Press.

Darwin, C. [1872] 1998. *The Expression of the Emotions in Man and Animals*. London: Harper Collins.

Doucet, M. 2007. 'Are your people fire fighters?' *Mechanical Engineering* 7: 28–9.

Ekman, P. 1985. *Telling Lies: Clues to Deceit in the Marketplace, Politics, and Marriage*. New York: Norton.

Ely, R. J. 1995. 'The power in demography: Women's social construction of gender identity at work'. *Academy of Management Journal* 38 (3): 589–634.

Featherstone, T. 2010. 'When the chairman underperforms'. *Company Director* 26 (6): 20–26.

Feindler, E. L. (ed.) 2006. *Anger-Related Disorders: A Practitioner's Guide to Comparative Treatments*. New York: Springer.

Francis, R. D. 1999. *Ethics and Corporate Governance: An Australian Handbook*. Sydney: University of New South Wales Press.

————. 2009. *Ethics for Psychologists*, 2nd ed. Oxford: BPS Blackwell.

Francis, R. D. and A. Armstrong. 2009. 'Meetings, morals and manners: Applications for the Corporations Act'. *Australian Journal of Corporate Law* 23 (1): 94–114.

Francis, R. D. and M. Mishra. 2009. *Business Ethics*. Delhi: Tata McGrawhill.

Gunther, N. 1987. *Debating and Public Speaking*. Newton Abbot: David & Charles.

Harzing, A. W. and J. van Ruysseveldt (eds).1995. *International Human Resource Management*. London: Sage.

Hinde, R. A. 1971. *Non-Verbal Communication*. Cambridge: Cambridge University Press.

Hodgetts, R. M. and K. W. Hegar. 2005. *Modern Human Relations at Work*. Mason, OH: Thompson South Western.

Isaacs, W. 1996. 'Basic components of a dialogue session'. In P. Senge, A. Kleiner, C. Roberts, R. B. Ross and B. J. Smith (eds),*The Fifth Discipline Fieldbook*, 357–64. London: Nicholas Brealey.

Janis, I. L. 1972. *Victims of Groupthink: A Psychological Study of Foreign Policy Decisions and Fiascos*. Boston: Houghton-Mifflin.

Janis, I. L. and L. Mann. 1977. *Decision Making: A Psychological Analysis of Conflict, Choice and Commitment*. New York: Free Press.

Jubb, P. B.1999. 'Whistleblowing: A restrictive definition and interpretation'. *Journal of Business Ethics* 21 (1): 77–94.

Kiel, G. and G. Nicholson. 2003. *Boards That Work*. North Ryde, NSW: McGraw-Hill.

Kiel. G., K. Kiel-Chisholm and G. Nicholson. 2004. *The ASX Corporate Governance Council's Principles: A Compliance Toolkit*. Milton, QLD: Competitive Dynamics.

Kotter, J. P. 1985. *The General Managers*. New York: Free Press.

Kurtz, P. D., K. E. Marshall and S. W. Banspach. 1985. 'Interpersonal skill-training research: A 12-year review and analysis'. *Counsellor Education and Supervision* 24 (3): 249–63.

Lang, A. D. 2006. *Horsley's Meetings: Procedure, Law and Practice*, 5th ed. Chatswood, NSW: LexisNexis.

Leblanc, R. and J. Gilles. 2005. *Inside the Boardroom: How Boards Really Work and the Coming Revolution in Corporate Governance*. Mississauga, ON: John Wiley.

Mantovani, G. 2000. *Exploring Borders: Understanding Culture and Psychology*. London: Routledge.

Margerison, C. and D. McCann. 1990. *Team Management: Practical New Approaches*. Sydney: Mercury.

Marx, E. 2001. *Breaking Through Culture Shock: What You Need to Succeed in International Business*. London: Nicholas Brealey.

McKenna, R. 1999. *New Management*. Sydney: McGraw-Hill.

Milhaupt, C. J. and M. D. West. 2004. *Economic Organisations and Corporate Governance in Japan: The Impact of Formal and Informal Rules*. Oxford: Oxford University Press.

Milligan, J. 2007. *The Penguin Guide to Chairing Meetings*. North Shore City, NZ: Penguin.

Mintzberg, H. 1973. *The Nature of Managerial Work*. New York: Harper & Row.

Moss Kanter, R. 1983. *The Change Masters*. London: Unwin.

Mosvick, R. K. 1971. 'Human relations training for scientists, technicians, and engineers: A review of relevant experimental evaluations of human relations training'. *Personnel Psychology* 24 (2): 275–92.

Muenjohn, N., A. F. Armstrong and R. D. Francis. 2010. *Leadership in Asia Pacific: Readings and Research*. Melbourne: Cengage.

National Association of Corporate Directors. 2001. 'Report of the NACD Blue Ribbon Commission Director Professionalism'. Washington, DC: National Association of Corporate Directors.

Nicholls, L. B. 2005. 'Inside an effective boardroom'. *Company Director* (online), December 2005: 60–63. Available from www.companydirectors.com.au (accessed 1 August 2010).

Parkinson, C. N. 1965. *Parkinson's Law*. Harmondsworth: Penguin.

Paul, K. 1995. *Chairing a Meeting with Confidence: An Easy Guide to Rules and Procedure*, 3rd ed. North Vancouver: Self-Counsel Press.

Pease, A. 1997. *Body Language*. London: Sheldon Press.

Pease, G. and K. McMillan. 1993. *The Independent Non-Executive Director*. Melbourne: Pro-Ned and Longman.

Reece, B. L. and R. Brandt. 2005. *Effective Human Relations, Personal and Organisational Applications*. Boston: Houghton Mifflin.

Renton, N. E. 2000. *Guide for Meetings and Organisations*, vol 2. Sydney: Law Book.

Russell, J. A. and J. M. Fernandez-Dols. 1997. *The Psychology of Facial Expression*. Cambridge: Cambridge University Press.

Schein, E. H. 1985. *Organization, Culture, and Leadership*. San Francisco: Jossey-Bass.

Senge, P. M. 1995. *The Fifth Discipline*. North Sydney: Random House.

Senge, P. M., A. Kleiner, C. Roberts, R. B. Ross and B. J. Smith (eds). 1996. *The Fifth Discipline Fieldbook*. London: Nicholas Brealey.

Sherif, M. and C. W. Sherif. 2009. 'Acceptable and unacceptable behaviour defined by group norms'. In M. Argyle (ed.), *Social Encounters*, 237–46. London: Aldine Transaction.

Standards Australia International. 2003. *Australian Standard: Corporate Governance AS 8000–2004*. Sydney: Standards Australia.

Stroh, L. K. and H. H. Johnson. 2006. *The Basic Principles of Effective Consulting*. Mahwah, NJ: Erlbaum.

Stuart, D. 2008. 'Through thick or thin'. *Company Director* 24 (8): 32–6.

Taylor, F. 1911. *The Principles of Scientific Management*. New York: Harper & Row.

Tricker, R. I. 1994. *Corporate Governance: Practices, Procedures and Power in British Companies and Their Boards of Directors*. London: Glover Press.

Tuckman, B. 1965. 'Development sequence in small groups'. *Psychological Bulletin* 63: 384–9.

Waldron, J. 1999. *The Dignity of Legislation*. Cambridge: Cambridge University Press.

Wan Yusoff, W. F. and A. Armstrong. 2010. 'Human Capital of Company Directors: A Study of Malaysian Public Listed Companies'. 2nd International Conference on Business, Technology and Engineering, IQRA University, Islamabad, 23–24 January 2010.

Wharton, T. 2009. *Pragmatics and Non-Verbal Communication*. Cambridge: Cambridge University Press.

Wood, J., J. Wallace, R. M. Zeffane, J. G. Hunt and J. R. Schermerhorn. 1998. *Organisational Behaviour: An Asia-Pacific Perspective*. Milton, QLD: Jacaranda Wiley.

Zimbardo, P. and J. N. Boyd. 1999. 'Putting time into perspective: A valid, reliable individual-differences metric'. *Journal of Personality and Social Psychology* 77: 1271–88.

INDEX